It's NEVER TOO LATE with

God

Carole Rucci

Packaged by WinePress Publishing, PO Box 428, Enumclaw, WA 98022. The views expressed or implied in this work do not necessarily reflect those of WinePress Publishing. Ultimate design, content, and editorial accuracy of this work are the responsibility of the author.

All Scriptures are taken from the King James Version of the Bible, except where noted. Many are author paraphrased.

Scriptures annotated by "AMP" are taken from *The Amplified Bible*, Old Testament © 1965, 1987 by The Zondervan Corporation. The *Amplified New Testament* copyright © 1958, 1987 by The Lockman Foundation. Used by permission.

Scriptures annotated by "NIV" are taken from the *Holy Bible, New International Version*®. Copyright © 1973, 1978, 1984 by International Bible Society. NIV and New International Version are trademarks registered with the United States Patent and Trademark office by International Bible Society. Used by permission.

© Song: "Laura" Lyrics by Johnny Mercer. Music by David Raksin. © 1945, [Renewed 1973] by Twentieth Century Music Corporation. All Rights controlled by EMI Robbins Catalog, Inc., [Publishing] and Warner Bros. Publications, U.S. Inc., [Print]. All Rights Reserved. Lyrics reprinted by permission of Warner Bros. Publications, Miami, FL 33014

© Song: "How Great Thou Art" 1953, S. K. Hine. Assigned to Manna Music Inc., 35255 Brooten Road, Pacific City, OR 97135. Renewed 1981. All Rights Reserved. Used by permission.

© Song: "Father, I Adore You" © 1972 Maranatha Music [Administered by The Copyright Company, Nashville, TN] All Rights Reserved. International Copyright Secured. Used by permission.

ISBN 0-9703608-2-7
Library of Congress Catalog Card Number: 2001-086781

This is dedicated to

Christine and Heather,

who give me reason to live

and to

my nephew, Billy, who kept encouraging

me over the years to write this book.

Acknowledgments

This is an official thank you to Heather, who was willing to "make due" while I was working on this project, and for letting me use my computer all that time.

A special word of thanks goes to my friend Sandy, who co-labored with me on the telephone for many hours, editing this book.

Finally, to all my other friends who helped get this into print by cheering me on, giving advice, proofreading, copying, supporting me in prayer, and giving financially.

Table of Contents

Introduction

*W*hen I decided to write this book, it was important for me to remember that the most significant things in my life were not the things that have happened or what I have learned by my intelligence, but what God has written on my heart. When a person comes to this understanding, his or her life becomes the kind of book that can be opened up and shared with others. Then it can be given away to whomever will receive it. It is important to remember that this is a story about a very ordinary person who serves an extraordinary God.

I firmly believe that all things do work together for good to them that love the Lord and who are called according to His purpose. I have endeavored to present some of those things to you, so that they may not only be for the edification of men, but to bear witness before heaven and all the powers of darkness that our God can be, and is, glorified through every one of our life experiences.

Whether the call of God comes early or late in your life does not matter. What does matter is how you respond. My call was somewhat delayed, but He has shown me it's never too late with God.

Out of the Mire

For I know the thoughts *and* plans that I have for you,
says the Lord, thoughts *and* plans for welfare *and* peace,
and not for evil, to give you hope in your final outcome.
—Jeremiah 29:11 (AMP)

*T*he words floated down from the platform, and once
more I felt that stirring feeling somewhere in the pit
of my stomach—or was it in the area of my heart?
The speaker was saying ". . .and I thank God that I came
from a wonderful Christian family. I was a preacher's kid
and was raised on the Word of God. . ." What was it that I
felt every time I heard someone say similar words? I don't
know what else to call it, so I wonder, is it possible to feel a
little jealous, but not have any harmful thoughts against
the person? Is it jealousy or is it just the longing in my
heart to know what it *could* have been like for me if *I* had
come from that kind of a family? Is this feeling any different than what a blind person must feel from time to time if
someone says to them, "How I wish you could see the sun-
set right now"? Inside, they must have that same feeling
and be saying to themselves, "Yes, so do I!"

Whatever the feeling is, that's what it's like for me at
times when I hear some Christian say that their whole family was saved and they were all involved in the work of the
Kingdom. I get a kind of longing in my heart, and although
my mouth doesn't move, my mind begins to formulate the
words, *How I wish that could have been me.*

When I think about all these beautiful families who have
spent years and years learning about the Lord and serving
Him, while a lot of us wallowed about in the mire of life

9

just trying to survive, it's then that I plug back into my inner on-going conversation with the Lord. I say, "God, I'm going to have to remember what the Bible says in Romans 8:28; that is, 'And we *know* that all things work together for good to them that love the Lord and who are the called according to His purpose.' So then, You must have had some good reason for the family You gave me and for calling me so late in life. But sometimes, Lord, I can't help thinking or feeling that if only I had heard Your call a little earlier, so many things might have turned out much differently. For one thing, I'm sure I would have made many different choices in life. Well, sometimes I don't understand anything You do, but I've learned by now that You know best, Lord." I wonder, dear reader, can you relate?

You see I didn't come from a warm, loving Christian family. Moreover, I was forty-nine years old when I asked Jesus into my heart and accepted Him as my Savior. It used to make me cringe inside when I thought about all the time that was wasted. It all seems to have happened too late in life. However, in the great big scheme of things (which only He can see and I can't,) although I got a really late start, it's better late than never. When I look at what a work He has done in me over these past seventeen years, it's hard to believe where I came from spiritually and in every other way. As the old cliché goes, "I may not be where I want to be and I may not be where I should be, but praise God, I'm not where I used to be."

Just thinking about the family I grew up in makes me shake my head and I almost have to laugh. Not that it was funny or amusing, because it wasn't. Pathetic is probably more like it. I was the youngest of three children born during a time called the Great Depression. It was difficult growing up through those early years, and there was little or no thought given as to why things were the way they were.

The emphasis was only on staying alive. As I look back, I realize that, as a family, we were really a mess. There was so much abnormal behavior that, in order to survive as children, we had to learn to make adjustments in our personalities in order to fit in. What is sad is that those adjustments were ingrained and eventually became part of our own personalities. Several years ago the buzz-word for a family like ours was *dysfunctional*, and from what I've read, and by every nuance and definition of the word, we definitely were "it." In fact, it is very possible that if Daniel Webster had known us he would have put our names and pictures next to the definition of the word in his dictionary.

It seems as though some things just do not change, because the Bible lists many families whose lives and behavior definitely fit into that same category. For starters, there was Adam, Eve, Cain, and Abel. Then there was the family of Abraham, Sarah, Ishmael, and Isaac. It goes on to tell us that the pattern continued with Isaac, Rebecca, Jacob, and Esau and carried right on to affect Jacob's children and all their families as well. When I come to think of it, we were really in very good company. In fact, right up to the present time, the world is still full of dysfunctional families, so we were not alone.

In the family I grew up in, in order to survive, you either learned to fight or you didn't *grow* up. Although it may seem odd, as children we laughed a lot, even in the midst of all the pain. In fact, laughing at things that weren't even remotely funny was one of our coping mechanisms. As a result, for most of my life people have said I'm a very funny person and a natural comedienne. With few exceptions, God has enabled me to see the humorous side of almost every situation, and sometimes even when I'm relating a sad incident, it seems to come out in such a way that the people listening to me are in tears from laughing. Probably being comical and having a keen sense of humor is just one of the natural by-products of growing up in a mixed-up family such as ours. I found that we all have our choices to make on how we are going to take life. We can either laugh at it or it gets the best of us. I was determined it wasn't going to get me.

Worrying about wounded psyches or whether our tender little spirits were being broken was not a priority with my parents. I remember one time asking my mother, "Mom, did you really want me when I was born?" She very matter-of-factly answered, "Of course not! You were born during the Depression. Who needed another mouth to feed?" That might have crushed me at one time, but now I can smile and say to the Lord, "I know it doesn't matter who did or didn't want me. *You* wanted me to be born! And You had a *reason* and a definite plan for my life. How come I never knew that in the midst of all the chaos, You were there, and You had Your hand on me?"

It had never occurred to me during all those years that God knew about everything that went on in my family. What a life-changing revelation it was for me to find out He did. Sometimes, in wonder, I said to Him, "You knew all my faults and all there was to know, and yet You still loved me! Who would have thought that some day You would speak through Your Word to let me know that before the foundation of the world You had set me apart to be holy? Me? Holy? Judging from the family *I* came from, who *would* have, or *could* have thought that—except You?"

It's true. Only He knew that some day I would be writing books, speaking at conferences, and that in the fullness of time, He would use all my feistiness to do spiritual warfare against the devil and teach others to do it as well.

There were five of us in our immediate family, which consisted of my father, mother, an older brother and sister, and me. In addition, I also had my mother's mother who was the most wonderful little grandmother in the whole world. She was the one who loved, nurtured, and affirmed us as children and was the kindest, most patient person I have ever known. During my preschool years, she always lived either with us in our apartment or very close to us in the same building. As the youngest, I was blessed because I got to spend the most time with her.

In my early childhood, we lived on the sixth floor of a tenement building on the Lower East Side of New York City in a cold-water flat. The bathtub was in the kitchen and had a big, enameled metal cover over it, with a shirred, calico skirt around its bottom. When we bathed, we put up a screen for privacy and heated up huge pots of water, either on the gas or coal-burning potbelly stove in the kitchen. On hot summer nights we slept up on the roof or on the fire escape, and in the winter we took red-hot coals from the fire and put them into long-handled bed warmers. In those days there were large, stone drinking troughs shaped like bathtubs on the sidewalks from which the wagon-pulling horses drank. We had an icebox, not a refrigerator, and the radio was the main source of entertainment.

In our neighborhood we had all kinds of people, with an assorted mixture of nationalities and religions. In addition to learning Italian from my grandmother, I also learned to speak a little Czechoslovakian and Chinese from some of our neighbors. Although all the people came from many different backgrounds, they had two things in common. They were all poor and most of them were angry. Fighting and beatings were a daily affair. It was an era when, if children were punched, kicked, or abused, nobody seemed to care, not even God. I grew up feeling that I didn't care much for a God who didn't care much about me.

My first awareness of a thing called death came while I was still very young. When one of our neighbors died very suddenly, I remember asking, "Why did she die, Mom? Can she ever come back? Where did she go?" It was then that I was told nobody knew why people died and, when they did, there was a place called heaven where the good people went and a place called hell for the others. In my mind I remember thinking, *Well, God, it seems You just like to wipe people out for no good reason. Is that what You're going to do to all of us someday when we least expect it?*

Sometimes when I went to the park, I delighted in crushing the big, black ants that ran back and forth along the walkways. In my total ignorance of God's true nature, I used to play and imagine that I was God, and every time I stepped on one of those ants, I said, "There. Gotcha! Just like God!" That's what I thought He was like! I really thought He enjoyed stomping out people the way I liked stomping out the ants. To me, God had no feelings, no motives. He was just deadly. What wretchedness of soul, and not the kind that comes from an awareness of God's awesome holiness, but the kind that springs from woeful ignorance of Him.

When I was about seven years old, we moved from the slums of New York City to Brooklyn. To me it was like being in the country. There were so many trees, and everything looked so green and beautiful. All the neat little houses with their lovely gardens and flowers used to make me think that if there really was a heaven, this must be what it was like. While heaven was something I had heard about, I didn't hold much hope of ever getting there. Judging from all the names we were called and the things that went on in our family, I was sure God didn't like me. The feeling was mutual. Still, I felt that even if I never got to heaven, this place served as a pretty good substitute for the time being.

Little did I know that some day I would come to under-stand that He had prepared a place for me and that "eye has not seen nor ear heard, nor has it even entered the imagination of man" the glories He has in store for us. That's His promise to me and to all those who have come to accept Him as their Savior. I'm so grateful that even if it seems as though my call was late in coming, with God it's really never too late. I can smile about it now because I realize that somehow, even from out of the mire, God is able to bring forth flowers.

Survival

...He who began a good work in you will carry it on to completion until the day of Christ Jesus.
—Philippians 1:6 (NIV)

As I approached my teens, the number one thing that kept me going continued to be survival, with no thought whatsoever about my eternal destiny. I was angry and determined. Often I would say aloud to whatever was out there, "You think all this is going to get me down? Well, you're wrong! Somehow I am going to stay strong and get control of my life, and nobody is going to stop me."

The abuse was still going on, but for some unknown reason my brother was never hit or even punished. I still have no explanation as to why the ill treatment was aimed only at my sister and me, but after talking with other women of Italian extraction, I have found the same was true in their cases.

Over and over again, how I thank God for my grandmother. Had it not been for her, there would have been little or no refuge at all. The woman was a saint. She loved us and prayed for us constantly, but there was not much more she could do to help. Although many years later I came to know Jesus as my "All in all," at that time, Grandma was the only anchor in the storms of my life.

It's not as though I had never heard about God's love for humanity. I used to think, *Well, maybe that's for some people, but I'm just not included. I know some kids are really loved and treated well by their parents, and I don't understand why we're not. It must be that some people were meant to enjoy life and others were meant to suffer. I guess that's it. And I guess I just belong to the latter group.* So I pretended it was all right and redoubled my efforts to survive.

Because of all that went on, the many strengths and weaknesses of our family members were all brought out in sharp contrast to each other. However, despite my determination to survive, a kind of confusion had set in. Somewhere along the way I never developed the ability to sift out and recognize the difference between what was good and should have been taken in to nurture me, or what was bad and should have been rejected as harmful. So I took in everything. By the time I was twelve, my own particular mental grid system through which I processed all incoming information, had already been warped and firmly stamped with the word *Reject*. Things were bad, but the worst was yet to come.

When I was sixteen years old, our family had gone to have a picnic at Lake Ronkonkoma on Long Island. My twenty-year-old brother and I decided to swim out to the float that was in the middle of the lake, neither one of us aware of the tragedy that was about to occur. I had started out first, and by the time I got to the float, I could barely pull myself up on to it. He was about thirty feet away, and as I lay there watching him swim toward me, he suddenly broke his stride. "Carole," he called out, "help me." His eyes were wide open as he sank beneath the surface of the water.

I watched the place where he went down and somehow I knew something terrible was happening. I sat up and began screaming his name and instinctively cried out, "Oh God, please help him, God, please." But he never came up. I jumped into the water and began swimming toward the spot, but there was no marker, no visual guide as to exactly where he had gone down. People on the beach heard the screams and began swimming toward us, but it wasn't until three hours later that his body was found about a hundred yards away. An autopsy showed that he suffered a massive heart attack and had died instantly. It was the direct result of his having had a strep throat infection two weeks before, and it had reactivated the rheumatic fever he had as a child. The aftermath of that incident was a living nightmare, because this time death had struck our family directly.

I don't believe it serves any good purpose now to stir up the whole pot of emotions of that day. Yet, I can still remember that all of the beatings and all the verbal abuse of the previous years faded by comparison to the pain I felt when I was told that the wrong person had died. When I look back, I wistfully say to the Lord, "How I wish I had known You at that time. What a difference it would have made for me to know You had a purpose for my life and my being alive wasn't due to some divine error. If only I had known that not only was Your plan unfolding for me, but that You were going to see me through it to the end."

Ironically, my brother's death brought about the first glimmer of spiritual life in the family. It was only as an after-effect that for the first time in my life I saw my mother praying and going to church. In some ways, the whole idea seemed so hypocritical, especially in view of her attitude towards me. Yet, it seemed to be helping her to get through the tragedy, so I decided to look into this thing called "religion" to see if I might find some solace in it as well. Of course, at the time I didn't know that religion couldn't do it, but what I really needed was a relationship with Jesus. However, survival was my goal, and I was ready to try anything.

To some degree it did help. Eventually I became a diligent churchgoer and got involved in various religious activities. Still, there was a feeling of emptiness that nothing seemed to be able to fill. Now I know that need was a God-shaped void only Jesus can fill. It was then that I first began seeking God. I decided to start reading the Bible and read it from cover to cover over the next few years. I had a next-to-nothing faith, so I had no insight, no spiritual understanding at all, of what I was reading. For me, the Bible was just another book, and this was just another project I was determined to finish.

Sometimes I wonder what exact process takes place inside of us when we're still very young and do not get the love and affirmation we need. Somehow we manage to survive, but what happens when we get a twisted message and are wounded and damaged by the very people who are supposed to love us? Why is it that we so readily embrace the lies, but have such difficulty receiving the truth? For me, until the truth of God's love became a reality, I viewed the world and all its circumstances through my own particular set of warped lenses. Somehow, my human spirit was so battered and bruised that my belief system told me not only was I rejected by man, but by God as well.

Now that I have read and studied the Bible, I have come to know it is all the work of the enemy. The devil is very real, and John 10:10 tells us "the thief has come to steal, to kill and to destroy." God means for us to have acceptance, affirmation, and approval. When we don't get these things from an early age, the enemy uses our natural longing for them to bait the trap so that we will do just about anything to get those needs met. Sadly, I've found that most often he uses the people closest to us to do his dirty work. Through them, he dangles the bait, and, to quote the old cliché, we "swallow it hook, line, and sinker."

For several years I searched for an answer as to why rejection becomes such an irrevocable part of our belief system. Once I tried to trace its origin through my own family's generational lines, and as I went further and further back, I finally realized that it must have started all the way back with Adam and Eve. As it is with us, although they were forgiven, there were still many consequences to their disobedience. Now I know that when they sinned, God didn't reject *them*, but because of His holiness and justice, He *had* to reject their *sin*. They were probably not aware that He only drove them from the Garden of Eden so they would not eat from the Tree of Life and live forever in that sinful state. Yet for them, I believe the seeds of rejection were sown, and the iniquity of their sin has continued to spill over from generation to generation onto all the children of Adam.

It is a known fact that we have genes through which we inherit certain physical traits from our ancestors. Still, I believe there has to be some kind of spiritual inheritance passed down as well. On the negative side, it is called *iniquity*, and I'm convinced that the feelings of rejection we all go through are a part of that iniquity. It is also probable that because of sin and guilt, even when we do hear the truth, we can't receive it.

Over the years and through my ministering to hundreds of women, I have found that while some families are better than others are, everybody suffers from rejection to some degree or another. With good reason I was no exception—and suffer I did! However, I was also a survivor, and one of the techniques I used was that in order to compensate for the feelings inside that I was never quite good enough, as I got older I worked hard, developed high standards, and became an overachiever in everything. By the time I was seventeen, I had already graduated from high school, and for the next several years I worked a full-time job at a bank during the day and went to college at night.

Maintaining a high average was not difficult for me, but instead of giving the glory to God, I gave myself the credit for all my achievements. I really didn't know any better. It is amazing how in our ignorance and pride we credit ourselves for our accomplishments until we find out that it is only by the grace of God that we are even able to draw our next breath.

There is an excellent teaching that says that rebellion, rejection, and the root of bitterness, which is unforgiveness, go hand in hand. Is it ever true! I can remember from when I was a very little girl that while I was being hit, I would count the blows and all the while I would be thinking, *I'll get you back some day. Oh, it may take me years to do it, but some day I will.* Then I would write the number down in a little notebook that I called my "hit book." Many years later, in a workshop on forgiveness, in my imagination I saw myself handing that little book over to Jesus, and the restoration of my soul began.

At the time, though, a tough attitude was part of my survival kit. I still knew nothing about God's love, and I especially never heard that He actually loved *me.* Even if I had, I probably wouldn't have believed it, anyway. How could I? The only message that had come across, wrong as it might have been, was that God didn't like me because I was unlikable, and He was someone Who would, when I least expected it, "get me."

Nonetheless, deep inside I was searching for God, and He knew it, even if I didn't. He alone knew the depth of my woundedness, and only He could heal it. There must be a certain cry that goes out from the heart that only God can hear, and what is even more amazing is that *His* heart is crying out in the same way for *us!* He planted the seed of longing in me, because all the while He was yearning for me to receive the love He wanted to give me. Isn't that incredible? And it's wonderful, too!

When I got older and began seriously reading and studying the Bible, it still took a very long time to believe God loved me. That's the whole key—*believing*—not just in our head, but in our heart. Over the years, I learned to use the Word of God to change my entire belief system. The Bible says, "You shall know the truth and the truth shall set you free." I'm so grateful I have been able to experience His love, because it was only when His love became truth to *me* that the process of being set free began.

During most of my youth, all my anger, self-sufficiency, and determination is what seemed to sustain me, but later on it proved to be the very thing that also jeopardized several of my adult relationships. I knew I had to let it all go, but when I heard other people talk about trusting God and letting go of the anger, I would cry to Him and say, "But, God, if I let go of my anger, I'm so empty inside that I won't have anything else to sustain me."

But God. . .Oh, how I love that phrase, "but God. . ." All by itself, it still means so much. Sometimes there are situations in life that seem absolutely hopeless to man, but God is always there and He steps in. In His perfect timing, He intervenes and changes the entire course of our lives. He certainly changed mine.

By His grace He has brought me into a whole other realm of life and love. The Word of God has been an incredible source of comfort and joy. I have learned that the words written in that book were written there for *me*, just as they were written there for you, dear reader.

I remember how my whole outlook was changed the first time I read Psalm 18. When I came to the sixteenth verse, I read: "He reached down from on high and took hold of me; He drew me out of deep waters. He rescued me from my powerful enemy, from my foes who were too strong for me. They confronted me in the day of my disaster, but the Lord was my support. He brought me out into a spacious place; He rescued me because He delighted in me." (NIV). When I read that last phrase, I began to cry and said, "God, *me?* You delighted in *me?* You mean there's something worthwhile in me that could possibly delight You? And there's something in You that thinks I was worth rescuing? Is that why You let me live that day? Oh, I know it's true! You were there with me all along. Imagine? It's all so wonderful I can barely take it in. You know me, and it doesn't matter what I came from or where I am. Thank You, thank You, God. You delighted in me. . .and You love me. . ." I cannot even describe the joy to you, nor what a difference it made in my life. It was another step in the restoration of my soul and an even greater step in the process of survival.

The Call of God

3

Deep calleth unto deep at the noise of Thy waterspouts.
—Psalm 42:7

*O*nce I heard about a mountain climber who was asked why he was attempting to climb a very hazardous mountain. He answered, "Because it's there, and it calls to me." I've also heard it said that there is a call to the sea and only certain people who have something of the sea in them can hear it. When they do, they must follow. So it was when God called me. Up until that time I was simply existing, caught up in the daily routines of life. Then, in some supernatural way, it was as though God plucked the spiritual strings of my heart, and something deep within my being resonated. He called, and I answered.

Whenever I read the phrase, "deep calleth unto deep," I understand it to mean that the very depth of God reaches out to grasp the very depths of us. When the realization finally came that in my own life there had actually been a deep yearning for God all along, I remember saying to Him, "I always hoped there was the *possibility* of Your loving me, even if I *was* unworthy. I guess You honored that attitude of my heart. Although I never even imagined it, all the while You were drawing me to Yourself. It never could have started from my end, because at the time I didn't even know You. Oh, I knew *about* You, Jesus, but I didn't know *You*. Now I do! It must have been a special work of love on Your part, because You sure had a lot of work to do before this instrument could be of any use to You. Are You smiling, Lord? I am."

God not only had a plan for my life, but His keeping power preserved me to be used for His special purpose. He also patiently waited for me to recognize Him as my Source, and it took many years for me to find out the hard way that without Him, I can't do a thing. I jokingly tell people, "With God, the harder the head, the bigger the hammer He has to use. Well, I must have had a very hard head, because He let me get plenty of knocks on mine before I answered His call."

I met my husband, Rudy, when I was twenty-five years old, and within six months we were married. We had three children in three years and, between the incredible busyness of being a parent and dealing with my own inner turmoil, it left little room for God in my life. Although I prayed and went to church every Sunday, I still knew nothing about having a relationship with Him. We were steeped in tradition and ritual, but not relationship.

However, it wasn't until I was in my forties that I first became aware of God's pull on my heart. I felt this strange longing deep inside of me, and every time I found myself thinking about Him, I began to cry. I would say, "I don't understand what's happening to me. All I know is that something is changing inside. What is it, God? What's happening?" It was the farthest thing from my mind to imagine that it was a call to holiness.

At the time, there was a small circle of women whom I considered to be my friends. Although I didn't quite understand it myself, I recall trying to share with them the change in my heart attitude. One afternoon when they were pushing me for an explanation, much to my own surprise, I finally blurted out, "I don't know what's happening to me, but all I know is that I want to be a saint." They burst out laughing because they thought I was making a joke. Sheepishly, I said, "Even I feel foolish using those words because the only thing I know about saints is that they have their pictures on little prayer cards with gold halos around their heads. And I know that's not what I meant, but it's true. Somehow, I want to be holy. I do! I want to be a saint." And I began to cry.

When the women saw me crying and they realized I was dead serious, their whole attitude changed. They stopped laughing and, to my horror, they became very angry with me. One of them jeered and asked, "Is *that* what you want? Let me tell you something, Carole. You've lost your mind! Who do you think you are, anyhow? What are you trying to do, be better than the rest of us?"

Through my tears I responded quietly, "No, I don't want to be better than all of you, I just want to be better than *I* am, that's all."

That woman never realized how prophetic her statement was. In fact, this was actually the first step to my losing the "mind of the flesh," as the Bible calls it, and putting on the "mind of Christ." I immediately became aware of the feeling that some day I would eventually have to separate myself from those women, but I managed to push the thought to the recesses of my mind. I actually spoke to that feeling and said, "Get out of here! No way will I ever do that. After all, these are my *friends*, and I *love* them. And *they* love *me!* Even if I wanted to, never would I have the strength to do something like that." As it turned out, I didn't have to worry about it for long because *they* dropped *me!* Abruptly!

It seems that a few days after that incident the women met together and came to a decision. One of them called me saying, "We have decided that we no longer want you to be part of our group. You've changed, and you no longer fit in. We're sorry, but that's the way it is." Then she simply hung up. So much for the fact that I thought they loved me. When I first got the call, the rejection I felt was so incredibly painful that for days all I could do was cry. But then a strange thing happened. I awoke one morning a week or so later with the feeling that a great weight had been lifted from me. It had!

In the years to come, it was so exciting for me to find the word "saint" over and over again in the Bible. When I realized that it referred to us and it meant the "called out ones," I rejoiced. One day, remembering the incident with those women, I smiled and whispered to Jesus, "You heard me that day, didn't You? You were there and You knew it was true." And, indeed He had. Somehow I had the distinct feeling He was smiling back.

As the years progressed, God undertook to make many changes in me. I was so thrilled the first time I read Philippians 1:6, which says, "He Who began a good work in you will carry it on to completion until the day of Christ Jesus." While I was no great surprise to God, in the making of *this* saint He really had His work cut out for Him. But. . .He is able!

The greatest work God did was in the area of forgiveness. For some reason, when I became a parent and felt such overwhelming love for my own children, the anger toward both my parents, which had been stuffed and denied for so many years, began to surface. Like a volcano emerging from beneath the sea, the pain and anger which was underneath, rose up in a torrent of rage toward them for all the love I had missed as a child. Most of it still had to be kept to myself because, at any age, disrespect would not be tolerated. The inner torment continued for years until, when I was forty-nine, I visited a church outside of my denomination and gave my heart to Jesus. Now, torn between feelings of vengeance and wanting to walk rightly with God, I was in agony.

After all, I was a Christian and the Bible said I was a new creation. I didn't know at the time that it was only "positionally" that I was justified, sanctified, and glorified. In my spirit all things were made new, but in my soul, that is, in my mind, my will, and my emotions, I was still carrying around a lot of excess baggage that had to be disposed of. Every time I read one of Jesus' teachings on forgiveness, there was a pull on my heart, and my soul was truly in torment.

Anger had always been a way of life for me, but I was not aware of just how much I had or what a stronghold it had on my life. Although I knew I had to forgive, I couldn't bring myself to do it. Or rather, I *wouldn't*. The bitterness and resentment I felt toward my parents seethed within me, until one day I broke. In agony I screamed out to God and finally acknowledged the pain beneath my anger.

Somewhere I had read that Jesus took our pain and our sorrows and that by His stripes we were healed, but I knew He couldn't take them from me unless I was willing to let them go. Between sobs I whispered a prayer, "Please, Jesus, take my pain and my anger. I can't deal with them anymore. I give it over to You. Please help me to forgive. I can't do it without You. But Jesus, I have to be honest, I'm still not ready to forgive them for *everything*, but I *am* willing to allow You to forgive them through me." That was only the beginning.

One of the keys that unlocks the door to freedom is believing and the other is forgiveness. I recognize the fact that forgiveness is not spiritual amnesia, but it *is* the exercise that allows the poison to drain from the wound. How I desperately needed to submit my will to God. How desperately I needed to forgive. The wonderful thing is that when I asked Jesus to help take the bitterness from me, the Holy Spirit immediately began that work inside of me. It didn't happen overnight, but slowly the thoughts that some day I would "get them back" began to be replaced with a true forgiveness and a genuine love. Now I know that time does not heal all wounds, but forgiveness does.

Over the years God gave me the grace to not only be able to pray *for* my parents, but I eventually had the privilege of leading both my father and my mother through the prayer of salvation before they went Home to be with the Lord. In the fullness of time, and through His love and mercy, I finally got to the place where Jesus was not only my Savior, He became the Lord of my life. He took the sword of vengeance from my heart and replaced it with the sword of His Spirit. Through the Word of God, I began to recognize Him as my true sustenance and strength.

I find it most amazing that God took the very thing I thought was the worst detriment to my spiritual walk, my anger and feistiness, and used it for His glory. Once I surrendered them to the Lord, they became powerful tools He used through me to fight our real enemy, the devil. In addition, He called me to write a book and to teach on the subject of spiritual warfare to thousands, not only through that book, but also through seminars and retreats.

I love to repeat Romans 8:28, and especially the King James Version, because it says, "And we know that all things work together for good to them that love God, to them who are the called, according to His purpose." For some reason that phrase, *"the called,"* made an enormous difference to me. It somehow made me feel very special to know that I am one of *"the"* called of God. Because I still need to feel special that way, I often quote that Scripture to myself and share it with others whenever I can.

It took a long time to break down the barrier to my being able to receive all the "love notes" from God that are written in the Bible. It enabled me to be thankful for all the people in my life which He used to help me respond to His call. You will hear about some of them in the following chapters.

So long ago God called and began a good work in me, and the spiritual cleansing has been an ongoing process ever since. To this day, He continually reveals other areas of my soul that are in need of healing. Jesus is still in the process of "setting the captive free," by renewing, restoring, and rebuilding me from the inside out. Once I began to learn the truth of Who God is, and who I am *in Him*, I was set free, and I am free indeed.

The Little Giant

I have been reminded of your sincere faith, which first
lived in your grandmother. . .
—2 Timothy 1:5 (NIV)

*G*randma, you'll never guess what I learned
tonight. . ." That was the way I often greeted this
special lady as I ran into her cozy little apartment. I
was going to college at the time and was so excited to have
someone with whom I could share the wealth of knowledge being opened up to me. To my utter amazement,
she would often respond, "Oh yes, *Carolina*. . ."
[Italian for *Carole*] and she would proceed to expand
and expound on the subject I was presenting to her.

She would then pour me a cup of the every-ready, pitch-
black demitasse coffee, and as I shared my newfound information with her, over and over again I was stunned to find
out how much of it she already knew. Grandma was self-
educated, and not only fully acquainted with the history of
western civilization, but she had read all the Greek and
Roman classics as well. There were many a night we sat
together at her kitchen table sipping coffee and discussing
Plato and Aristotle—she in Italian, and I in English. What
an amazing person she was, and I cannot possibly tell the
story of my life without devoting at least one chapter to
this remarkable little woman.

Her real name was Mary, but to me and to everyone else
she was "Little Grandma." She was only four feet, eight
inches tall, but only on the outside. Inside she was a giant.
She looked like so many of the other little old ladies of her
time, modestly dressed with her hair tied in a bun. But the

similarities stopped there. Underneath the surface, there was more love, wisdom, and knowledge than most of the people I have met, and she was unlike anyone I have ever known.

In stirring up my remembrances of her, I found a noteworthy similarity between the time frame of my grandmother's life and my own. Grandma was born in 1885, and when she was fifty years old I was born. One hundred years later, almost to the day, my own granddaughter, Heather, was born in 1985 when I was fifty years old. My grandmother raised me for part of my life and was loving and nurturing to me, and I, too, have been lovingly raising my granddaughter since she was a baby. It's nothing remarkable, yet it is interesting. Coincidence? No. God-ordained.

I have never met a more even-tempered, patient person than she was. Until she died at the age of eighty-seven, I never once heard her say a negative thing about anyone in all those years. We shared many a good laugh, though, because she had a quick wit and a great appreciation for slapstick humor. Grandma's outstanding characteristic was her ability to love with no strings attached. She never condemned anybody, although there was plenty of reason for condemnation. Hugging was another one of her great attributes. She was a plump little woman, and whenever I nestled into the softness of the wonderful hugs she gave, I could feel her love pouring out and filling my being. Oh, how I needed and cherished those hugs.

Another outstanding characteristic was that Grandma was a praying woman. She prayed all the time, and I often heard her whispering the name of Jesus as she went about her chores. For many years my sister and I shared the same bedroom with her, and I can remember hearing her drop off to sleep every night whispering over and over again, "*Jesu mio, misericordia,*" which means, "My Jesus, mercy."

In fact, Grandma never ever walked out the door without first saying, "*Jesu mio, Tu avanti ed Io appresso,*" which means, "My Jesus, You go first and I'll follow."

The immense wealth of knowledge she had, along with a great sense of humor, made her a wonderful storyteller. There was no television in those days to rob from family life, and I remember that as children there was many a night we would sit on the floor around her rocking chair just listening to her tell all kinds of wonderful tales. She also told us some stories from the Bible, but to me they were just accounts about other people and other times. I never made any real connection to God and never thought of applying them to myself. If I had, then I would have had to ask why He wasn't there to protect us, and I had enough targets for my anger. I'm sure it was only her prayers so many years before that led to my eventually coming to know Jesus and accepting Him as my Savior and Lord.

During my preschool years, there was a period of time when Grandma moved to her own apartment in another part of Manhattan. I have no idea how or why I got to live with her for many months at a time, but the sweetness of those days will forever be etched in my memory. As children, probably the greatest contribution she made in our lives was the fact that she always affirmed us. Even when we pushed her to her limits of patience and she had to reprimand us, it was always done with love. Then, we always "made up" with a great big hug.

Grandma read at least one book a week, and though she could read English, she preferred reading in Italian. Every few months she would go over the *New York Times'* Best Sellers' List and decide which books she wanted to read in Italian. The New York Public Library used to send her specially printed postcards, which she would mail back to them to request a particular book. When the Italian translations came through, it was always a treat to go with her to the Forty-Second Street Branch of the Library, because it was always followed up by a trip to the Automat.

Maybe some of you readers are either too young or you have never been to New York, nor heard of Horn and Hardart's Automat. For the benefit of those who missed the wonderful experience of going there, it was probably the very first edition of an automated fast food cafeteria. It was not just a place to eat, it was a place where you could have fun and one on which to build a memory.

The room was huge and all the walls were lined with hundreds of little compartments containing individual portions of every kind of delicious food and desert. Each compartment had a coin slot that took only nickels. You had to put the money in, turn a little knob, and the door would pop open. You never saw the people behind the walls, but every few minutes all the doors in one particular section would snap shut and the shelves would rotate. When the compartments reappeared, they were restocked with food all over again.

When we were young, each month my brother, my sister, and I took turns going to the Automat with Grandma. Sometimes, when we all went there together, she gave each of us a whole dollar bill, which was a lot of money. We would then exchange the dollar for twenty nickels at a big, circular booth in the middle of the room, and scatter in every direction, buying enough delicious food to fill our bellies for a week and have money left over. In those days, for one nickel you could buy a piece of pie, cake, or any other desert. For ten cents, you could get a large dish of vegetables or a huge portion of mashed potatoes with a well in the middle filled with delicious brown gravy. For a quarter, you could buy a large chicken potpie, sliced turkey with sweet potatoes, or a chicken quarter. The food and the memories of those times are still sweet to the taste.

Grandma was not only good, smart, funny, and generous, but she was spunky as well. When she was eighty-four, she fell and broke her hip and had to have all the necessary surgery that comes with that kind of an injury. I was with her the day she was leaving the hospital and a young doctor was there at her bedside, trying to explain all the instructions that had to be followed once she got home. When he got to the part that he had ordered a wheelchair for her use, she interrupted him and said in her broken English, "No! I no want no wheelchair. No! If you give-a me wheelchair, I no walk-a no more. If you no give-a me wheelchair, I know I gotta walk. And I walk!" The doctor looked at me, I nodded, and he grinned and canceled the wheelchair.

True to her words, she did! She was so proud of herself as she moved around using her walker. It was really funny to the rest of us to watch her show off when my mother wasn't looking. With a little grin of satisfaction on her face, she would push the walker aside and cross the room without it. What a great determined little person she was!

Throughout my life, Grandma and I had a very special relationship. It's not as though she favored me over my sister or brother, it's just that she had the capacity of making each one of us feel as though we were the most special and loved people in the world to her.

Even as an adult, when I needed her she was always there for me. Sometimes I would nestle into her and she would pet my head and face as she did when I was a child. I remember her doing that when my own four-year-old daughter, Laura, died. Grandma just held me and we both wept together.

Some people come across the paths of our lives and their footprints leave an indelible mark. Grandma was one of them. It was a privilege to have known her. As a child, I loved her dearly. I still do. Thank you, God, for Grandma. I know that little giant was a very special gift to me from You.

A Slow Train

What is your life? You are a mist that appears for a little while and then vanishes.
—James 4:14 (NIV)

*O*nce upon a time, there was a girl named Laura. We gave her that name because of the hauntingly beautiful song by that name, which both my husband and I had always loved. Not only is the music beautiful, but all the words remind me of our own Laura. The last line of that song says, "That was Laura, but she's only a dream." That's all she is now, only a dream and a memory. Yet, for a wisp of time, she was really ours.

Laura was born in 1961, just eleven months after my husband and I were married, and she was wanted and loved from the very first moment she nestled deep within my body and shared my heartbeat. Even as a newborn baby, it seemed as though she never slept. She was awake for eighteen hours a day, and most of those hours she spent screaming because of colic. Any parent who has gone through it with a newborn knows what a nightmare that can be. Sometimes when Laura *was* quiet, I would tiptoe into the room to peek at her, only to find her little eyes wide open, looking all around. As her life progressed, there were so many other things that were not quite right that it finally became apparent she had come into this world with some very serious health problems.

The grand mal seizures began when Laura was six months old, and after having a whole battery of neurological tests done, she was diagnosed as having idiopathic epilepsy. The doctors explained that it meant there was no known cause. She had one of those rare cases of epilepsy that could not be controlled, even with medication. We were never able to find the root cause of the problem because those were the years before space-age technology gave us the kind of sophisticated tests we have today. To add to the horror, we found out through all the testing that she also had Cystic Fibrosis.

I remember feeling my head reel as the doctors droned on as to what we could expect as she got older. None of it gave any hope for a normal life or future for Laura. While I wept over the news, my husband got angry. He could not, and would not, accept either the diagnosis or the prognosis. I don't suppose anybody really knows how to handle that kind of terrible news. As young parents we certainly didn't. Apart from the sorrow, the most frustrating part of the situation was watching her suffer and not having any control over what was going on. It was not as though there was some tangible thing we could fight or really do something about. For me, it took having a child like Laura to bring the first glimmer of acknowledgment that I wasn't in control of things, but that Someone else *was*. In ways only God can do, He used this very circumstance to bring about a necessary change in me and in my thinking.

Each day my husband and I said every prayer we knew. Although I didn't really know how to pray for healing as I do now, I'm still not sure it would have made a difference. Despite all the care, tears, and prayers, it was somehow God's will to take Laura Home a few months before her fourth birthday. Some people have argued with me that it's *never* God's will to take a child Home. Maybe not. We really don't know all the answers, but children do die. Although it is true that it is the work of the enemy to steal, kill, and destroy, it is still God's sovereign will that allows it to happen. After years of asking the unanswerable question,

"Why?" I no longer do that. I've learned to find peace and rest in God's goodness, wisdom, and sovereignty, regardless of the circumstances. Peace came late, but it came.

Laura's life was brief, but not in vain. I like to think of God as the Great Economist, although you will never find that name applied to Him in the Bible. The fact is, although we cannot understand the "why?" of it, no life experience is ever wasted with Him, nor is it without reason. That was true in Laura's case. Through the painful times we learned how to love at a depth of which neither my husband, nor I, had been capable before. We became thankful for everything. By the time Laura was three years old, we had two more daughters born to us, Christine and Jacqueline. As we watched those children grow and develop, we became intensely grateful for every day of good health and every skill they were able to achieve. We never, ever again took anything for granted.

Every day had its own set of challenges. There were so many trials, so many sorrows to go through, but still we managed to laugh and have some happy times with Laura. They were few and far between and that made them even more precious to us. There were special times with her, too, because when her complete helplessness came, it allowed us to become a part of each other in a way nothing else could.

I can remember one incident in particular with Laura when all the seizures that wracked her body began to take their toll on her brain. Life and all its pleasantries seemed to be passing her by. During a family Christmas get-together, I caught Laura in her familiar pose, her little head tilted to one side leaning against her hand, and a blank little look in her eyes. I was hurting so badly for her as I knelt down beside her playpen. I looked into those beautiful brown eyes and asked, "Laura, baby, do you know that there's a whole world going on around you? Do you know it's Christmas? And that we're your family? And these are all your cousins? What do you think about in your little head? *Do* you think at all? *Can* you think?" I thought, *She's missing out on so many things in life, and it's not fair.* My heart was breaking, and I began to weep.

While I was crying, our eyes met. My breath caught, because suddenly it was as though a veil had lifted in Laura's eyes, and for an instant, a look of knowing, all knowing, came over her. A strange and beautiful smile, which I had never seen before, spread across her face. I spoke, and it was almost as though I was talking to her inner spirit. "Or do you know more than any of us will ever know?" I asked. "Are you so close to God that you understand all things better than we do because you haven't been contaminated by the world around us?" While I was still speaking, the look was gone the way it came. I never felt sorry for her that way again. It taught me never to judge someone else by a lack-luster look in their eyes or to ever think I know what is going on inside another person. I reached over and drew Laura close to me. I kissed her little face and, as best she could, she returned it.

We were always a very affectionate and demonstrative family, but Laura never really learned how to kiss. Not as we know a kiss. Most people have never had reason to consider how much coordination it takes to do the simplest task. However, it is a known fact that when the motor part of the brain is not functioning properly, the person can think about doing something but cannot coordinate the thought with the action. When Laura tried to kiss us, she would simply lay her mouth and tongue against our cheek or hand. I thank God for the gift of memory, because if I close my eyes, I can still feel that wet little warmth on my skin and I am eternally grateful.

The Bible tells us that our life is like a vapor that appears for a little time and then vanishes away. It is so true. We are only pilgrims and sojourners passing through this life on our way to eternity. Once more that song comes to mind because it has words that seem to fit Laura's little life perfectly. One line says, "And it was Laura, like a train that came passing through. . ."

To me, that's what her life was like, a little train just passing through. Only Laura was not like most of the others. Most people come huffing and puffing through life filled with so much noise and self esteem, they remind me of super-speed express trains that never stop to pick up passengers because they're too busy on their own frenetic schedules. No, Laura was a slow train, slightly disabled, that picked up people and carried them along, giving and receiving love at every stop along the way.

Does a train ever know how may lives it touches on its run? Of course not. Neither did Laura. She never knew on her short journey just how many other lives she touched. There were people who hadn't prayed for years, but they prayed for her because her little light had shined in the dark places of their hearts. It's as though the Lord used her as a lamp through which He shed His light onto everyone around her. In the darkness of the tunnel, every inch was a hard-won victory, but there was Light at the end of that tunnel—and Love. She went back to the Lord and made it Home the same way she came in, following His light.

Every once in a while I dream of Laura, and sometimes it seems so real that I wake up smiling, thinking I'm going to be able to go into the next room and see and talk with her. Then the disappointment sets in as I realize it was only a dream.

There are six other family members who are now with Laura in that heavenly realm. I am so glad He has kept me here because it seems He still has lots of work for me to do. Yet, how I look forward to that glorious day when I will see all of them again. I know that when I do see Laura there, she will be perfect, whole, healed, and radiating the glory of the presence of the Lord. And that's not just a dream—it's a promise!

Jacqueline's Gift

You knew me when I was knit together in my mother's
womb.
—Psalm. 139:13 (AMP)

S ometimes in life a blessing comes our way and we
can't figure out why. This is what happened when God
sent my granddaughter, Heather. She is such a joy that
I remember saying to God a long time ago, "I have no idea
what it might have been, but somewhere in my life I must
have done something pretty wonderful for You to have given
me this gift. I guess You knew there would come a time
when we would need someone special, and You gave us to
each other."

This special "gift" came through our youngest daughter, Jacqueline. Thirteen years ago she left her two-year-old
little girl at our house for what was supposed to be a weekend visit, and Heather has been with me ever since. When
Jacqueline reached her eighteenth birthday, both her father
and I had become painfully aware that a serious drug problem was at the bottom of the drastic changes taking place
in her personality and behavior. We probably should have
had a revolving door installed in the front of our home
because from time to time she would leave the house and
not return for days, weeks, or sometimes, months.

Whenever Jacqueline did come home, I was usually so
happy to see her that I didn't dare ask where she had been,
or any other question I knew would not get me an honest
answer. I had not yet come to a place of being able to apply
the very difficult rules of "tough love." Oh, I knew some of
them, but I avoided using them, because most of the time

they involve a lot more pain for the parent than they do for the child. I didn't want having to deal with any more pain than I was already feeling.

Occasionally, Jacqueline would come home and stay for weeks or even months at a time. When she did, she knew the house rules and would stick to them for as long as she could. These rules involved respect for us, decent hours, coming to church on Sunday, no drinking, no drugs, and no "druggy" friends coming or calling. During those times, we were actually able to function as a loving family once again, and it was good.

A special time for all of us was when she found out she was expecting a baby and came home to stay for the full term of her pregnancy. Jacqueline came to church with her father and me regularly and spent hours at a time reading the Bible. Toward the end of her pregnancy, when the usual discomforts prevented her from sleeping well, I often found her sitting in the living room late at night reading her Bible out loud. I could hear her talking to the baby inside of her, saying, "Now, baby, we're up to John, chapter fifteen," or whatever chapter she happened to be up to and then she would continue reading.

I believe that hearing the Word of God during all those months had a profound effect on Heather. Not only did God know *her* before she was born, but from hearing His Word while she was still in her mother's womb, *she* had already begun to know *Him*. It did something special for her. The seeds of faith and love were sown and have been producing fruit throughout her life. Like all children, she is a precious gift from God. She has not only been a special blessing to me, but she is well liked and loved by many other people as well.

Time and time again, I have witnessed a loving obedience and a servant's heart in Heather that can only come from a love for God and His ways. I love how Psalm 40 says "You have given me the capacity to hear and obey. . .I delight to do Your will, O my God; yes, Your law is within my heart." (Psalm 40:6,8 AMP). From the time she was a little girl, that has always seemed to be part of Heather's thinking process. I believe it is a special grace given to her by God.

Soon after Heather's birth, Jacqueline went back into her life of drugs, and within a year or so, found she could no longer give proper care to her child. As her own life began spiraling downhill, she would call us every few weeks and ask if we would please come and pick up the baby. At the time, she was living in New Jersey, and Rudy and I would drive to whatever address we were given and keep Heather with us until her mother came to pick her up again. It became harder and harder to let Heather go back into only-God-knows-what kind of life she had there and I would cry for days afterwards. The day finally came when Jacqueline left Heather with us and never came back for her. In fact, she never, ever came back.

The permanent separation was terribly painful for Heather. It was very difficult trying to explain to such a little child why she could no longer see her mother. As each situation came up, I continually prayed to God for wisdom to handle her pain. True to His Word in James 1:5, He gave wisdom abundantly. When Heather asked me a question about her mother, I made sure not to give more information than was absolutely necessary. I took care not ever to say anything negative about Jacqueline but, at the same time, at whatever level I thought she could understand, I did not glamorize her mother's situation or deny any of the facts. To the best of my ability, I tried to let Heather know there wasn't anything wrong with *her*, but that Jacqueline was the one with the problem. It was important that she did not see herself as the cause of her mother's actions or behavior.

As the weeks went by, she often heard me using the term *abandonment* in connection with the procedures in becoming her legal guardian. Heather had an extensive vocabulary for a child her age, and she began telling anyone who asked that her mother had abandoned her. When she did, the people's mouths would drop open or their eyes would well up with tears. It began to upset me terribly that she was being stigmatized, even to herself, as a victim of abandonment. All I could do was pray.

One day I tried explaining to Heather that when a person abandons someone else, they don't care about the welfare of the other person, they just walk away and never look back. "The difference with your mommy," I said, "is that she *wanted* to keep you, but she couldn't keep you because she has very big problems. She didn't give you up because she doesn't care. She loved you from when you were the tiniest little baby inside of her." My heart was breaking to see the terrible sadness on Heather's face as I continued. "When she knew she could no longer take care of you the way she should, *because* she loved you so much, she gave you to Grandpa and me. That's because she knew how much *we* love you, and that we would always take the very best care of you. That's altogether different from not caring. It's not that your mommy doesn't love *you*, Heather, it's that she doesn't love *herself* enough and doesn't want to do anything to make herself better." At whatever level she could understand, these reassuring talks always seemed to help ease the pain.

With God's help and guidance, I did whatever I could do to help us get over those very difficult times. We prayed, sang songs to Jesus, and praised the Lord together, but it was the Holy Spirit Who did the inner healing we needed.

I say "we" because Rudy and I needed as much healing as Heather did. In fact, this whole situation dealt him such a devastating emotional blow and he grieved so deeply that, other than when he was with Heather, almost nothing was able to lift him out of his depression. Rudy's health was effected as well, and he began to fail to the point that just a little over a year after we got her, he died very suddenly of a heart attack.

Five years passed and when Heather was seven years old, I legally adopted her. At the time, I didn't know how she would feel about it, and I hesitated asking her until the week before the adoption. When I did, she sobbed with joy and said, "Oh, Grandma, now I can have a real mother like everyone else. Now we'll be a family." We had a huge party to celebrate the occasion and a cake that had written on it, *"We Are Family."*

Heather never did see her mother again. For the first couple of years, Jacqueline called occasionally on holidays or for Heather's birthday. Each time she would promise to visit and bring presents, and Heather would be continually disappointed because she never showed up. Watching Heather go through all the disappointment and pain finally got me to the point that I told her when Jacqueline called again, she was not allowed to speak to her. It was after two-and-a-half years of not having heard from her at all and only weeks after the adoption, that Jackie finally called in June of 1992.

I was in the backyard when I heard the telephone ring, but Heather was in the house and picked it up. Suddenly she came running out to me, wide-eyed and screaming, "Grandma, my mommy is on the phone. She said she called to talk to me. Oh, Grandma, I said 'hello,' and I want to talk to her some more but you said I'm not allowed to. Can I, Grandma? Can I, please. . .?"

My heart was pounding. After all, Jacqueline was still my daughter, and I still loved her. I had never stopped praying for her, and it had been so long since I had heard anything that for some time I had begun wondering whether or not she was alive. A surge of joy came over me to know that she was indeed alive. Suddenly, overriding my own thoughts and feelings about Jacqueline, I was struck by the awareness of Heather's incredible obedience. It had transcended her own deep needs and desire to talk to her mother.

Rallying my inner strength I answered, "Yes, of course you can talk to her, but first let me say a few words."

Heather held the kitchen phone while I went into the bedroom to use the extension. She understood she had to wait until I said she could talk. "Jackie," I said, "I'm so happy to hear your voice. And I know you called to talk with Heather, but first I have to ask you to please not make any promises to her you can't keep. I don't want her to be hurt or disappointed. I'll let you talk with her first and then, if you want, we can talk, okay?"

She agreed and Heather got on the phone. They talked for a moment or two while I listened, and then I heard Heather ask her mother, "Mommy, will you please hold on for a minute. There's something I have to do."

Jackie and I were holding on in silence when we heard loud, thumping sounds accompanied by the sound of Heather's voice shouting on the top of her little lungs. "What is she doing?" Jackie asked.

"I don't know," I answered. "Let me go see."

As I walked into the living room, there was Heather leaping in the air, with both arms extended over her head, shouting "Thank You, Lord, for answering my prayers. I love You, Lord, for bringing my mommy back to me. I love You. . .I love You. You are so good to me. Thank You

. . .thank You. . .thank You, Lord." A huge lump began to form in my throat and I couldn't speak.

Stunned, I stood there in silence, overwhelmed at the heart of this loving little child. Jackie had heard her and realized what Heather was doing, and I could tell she was touched as well. I know it is what we are all supposed to do but, once more, I was in awe that Heather actually put aside the joy of the moment to give thanks and praise to God first. This is the kind of loving obedience the Lord desires from all of us, but she didn't know that. She just did it without being told. It came from the depths of her heart. Only when a person knows the absolute reality of a loving God can such obedience be engendered.

Heather returned to the phone and wept with joy throughout the rest of the conversation with her mother. When she finished, Jackie and I talked for some time. I, too, was filled with joy at being able to talk with her again, but it was also with incredible sadness that I realized she had called because she knew she was dying.

During the next few months, Jacqueline spoke with Heather a number of times and sent several packages containing lots of pretty things little girls like. Heather keeps them in her "treasure box" and takes them out from time to time just to look at them and remember her mother.

Jacqueline died three months later. However, because the door of contact had been opened once more, there were times when the pain of missing her became too much for both of us to handle. Other than huddling very close to each other, there was not much else we could do. I would hold her and rock her in my arms and together we would both cry out our pain and anguish.

During those terrible times, the Holy Spirit inspired me with a way to help Heather deal with the pain. First, I reminded her that the Bible tells us angels were created to do the will of God. Then, that whatsoever we ask the Father in Jesus' name, believing, it would be done for us. We created a little ritual, and this is what we did: she would begin by asking, "Father God, will You please send an angel down to bring some love and kisses back to heaven to give to my mommy?" She knew and believed He had heard her, so she would add, "Now, Father, would You please ask the angel to stand in front of me and hold out his hands?" Then with her little hand, she would make the motion of taking portions of love from her heart and would put them in the angel's hand. Next she would purse her lips and make little kissing noises against her fingertips as she added a bunch of kisses to her cupped hand. Finally, she would give them to the angel standing in front of her and pray once more, "Father God, in Jesus' name, please ask the angel to take these kisses to my mommy and tell her that I love her very much." Her lips trembled as big tears rolled down her cheeks. My lips trembled, too. I'm sure the Father's heart was melting with love for her, and I believe He honored her prayer. Not only did Heather get enormous peace, but it helped me, too, because I threw in a couple of kisses myself.

To finish it off, the last step was to reverse the procedure and ask for kisses to be delivered from heaven back to Heather. I would reach out and take them from the invisible angel's hand and with my fingers, place them all over Heather's face and lips. The smiles were worth all the effort.

Heather was taught God's Word, and she learned to apply it to every situation in her life from a very early age. One evening we were watching a Christian video of the testimony of a dynamic young minister who had himself been given up as a baby. As we watched, I suddenly heard a sob coming from her direction. Quickly I shut off the tape as she ran to me, burying her face in my chest. "What is it?" I asked, "Heather, what's going on inside of you?"

"Oh, Grandma," she answered, weeping, "I was just thinking about what that man was saying and I thought about my mommy. You know how much I've cried that she left me when I was little? Well, I was thinking that if she hadn't left me with you I never would have come to love the Lord the way I do. Look at how much you have taught me about God. Who knows where I would be right now if I were still living with my mommy." Suddenly she looked up through her tears and her face broke into a huge smile as she added, "You know, Grandma, this really is a Romans 8:28, isn't it?" Praise God! The Word of God *is* alive and it ministers life to those who believe it.

From time to time Heather still gets sad and cries about her mother. As she gets it out and releases the pain, I remind her of all the wonderful promises God has made, especially that He has prepared a place for us. We both have the solace of knowing Jacqueline made her peace with the Lord before she died and she is already in that place. Heather also knows that some day she will see her mother again, and she's whole, healed, blessed, and in the presence of the Lord. Some day we will all be together, never to be separated again. What incredible comfort there is in that thought. It enables me to smile in anticipation and say, "What a day that will be!"

Who can know what joy or pain will come when we bring a child into the world and give them the gift of life? Even with all the grief and sadness, it is with a heart full of gratitude that I can thank God for Jacqueline. Not only for the love *we* shared with each other, but for Jacqueline's gift.

An Act of Mercy

Oh, give thanks to the Lord for He is good; For His mercy
and loving-kindness endure forever.
—Psalm. 118:1 (AMP)

*D*o you ever wonder where we would all be if it were
not for the incredible mercy of God? Most of us
probably wouldn't even *be* here! Have you ever
looked around at some of the things going on in the world
and said, "Now, if *I* were God, I'd. . .", and then later thanked
God that you are *not?* I have. I'm sure lots of other people
have, too. Can you imagine if we made decisions and did
things according to our emotions without the wisdom and
loving-kindness of the Lord? I shudder to think what this
world would be like, were it not for His mercy.

In the study of human emotions, it is a fact that whether
or not a person has had a good, nurturing relationship with
their father, profoundly affects their relationship with every other person in their life. This was certainly the case
with me. For many years the lack of nurturing from my
father not only affected my relationships with other people,
but for quite a long time it even hindered my relationship
with God.

There is really no point in trying to glamorize my feelings toward my dad for most of my life. Suffice it to say
they were definitely not good, with plenty of reason. However, the Holy Spirit began to do a work in my heart that
enabled me to forgive and eventually come to love him. I
don't think it serves any purpose to go into detail about
issues I have already dealt with and that have been put to
rest between my father and me. Still, I find that sometimes,

in order to validate where I am and what I am feeling, I have to take a realistic look back at what the conditions were that contributed to the shaping of my life. I need to see where I *was* and how God's love and mercy brought me to where I *am* today.

Sometimes when I hear other people talk lovingly about their fathers, it makes me sad to say that I was almost fifty years old before I was able to say the words, *I love you,* to mine. The first time I said those words to him, he could not even respond. After all, he had never heard them from me before. Instead he just shifted uncomfortably, cleared his throat, and looked away. About a month later when I said it the second time and he didn't respond, I asked him, "Did you hear me, Dad?"

"Yeah, I heard you," he said, his gruff voice softening a bit. The walls that had been built up between us for years were beginning to crack. The third time I said the words, *I love you, Dad,* he answered, his voice thick with emotion, "I love you, too, baby." The walls had come down.

Coming to a place of loving my *human* father came only after I began to realize the love of my *heavenly* Father. Then I was able to begin forgiving and loving my earthly one. It was my *real* Father's love for me that began to melt the walls I had built around my heart as a protection from being hurt. When I came to know Him, I was willing to put myself in a position of vulnerability. I knew I could always run to Him for comfort and He would never hurt me. You have no idea what it meant to know that I could come to Him and call Him, "Abba, Daddy. . .*my Abba.*"

When I truly understood the message that I had been forgiven of all my sins and my eternal salvation was purchased by Jesus at the Cross, it became a vital necessity for me to share it with my family, especially with my father. From that day on I was on fire to become a soul winner, a call that has not diminished to this day. Sadly, most of us have found it is far more difficult to witness to our own families than it is to witness to strangers. Nevertheless, every chance I could I just kept pressing in with mine.

The goal and focus of my prayers were for my father's complete outlook to change and that some day he would come to know and accept Jesus. Every time I brought up the subject of God, he would wave me away with his hand and say, "Naaaaa . . .don't give me that nonsense. There's no God, no heaven, and no hell. They just don't exist. All that happens when you die is that someone buries you, and it's all over." As dismal as that thought is, it really didn't seem to bother him any. Well, it bothered me plenty.

My dad wasn't educated enough to be called an atheist, and it's almost comical to say that he didn't even qualify as a heathen, because at least heathens believe in *some* god. He didn't believe in *anything!* For several years, I kept trying to share the gospel with him, to move him to say a prayer that would eventually bring him into the same love relationship with Jesus that I had. In fact, whenever I brought up the subject, he still poo-pooed the thought of anything existing after this life. One day he eloquently stated, "I've told you this before. When you die, they put you in a hole, and then the worms eat you. And that's the end of it."

All I could say to him was, "Well, isn't *that* a happy thing to look forward to!" As if his philosophy was not dreary enough, it made me shudder to think at least he had one part right, the part about the worms, but all the other things awaiting him at the end of this life would be a lot worse than that. So, I kept trying.

Since he had no foundation or basis on which to even anchor a prayer, it was hard to get him to pray. He simply didn't believe there was anybody "up there." Every chance

I had I would talk to my father about the Lord, but nothing seemed to sink in. One day I asked him, "Daddy, would you at least *try* to say a prayer? Just say these words, 'Jesus, I don't believe You are real, but I'm trying to believe. And I don't believe any of the things she says about You. But, if You *are* real, will You please show Yourself to me in a special way?'" Of course, on my end I knew that Jesus is all I could ever think He is—and more. Because my father was, among other things, a gambler, I told him it was a "safe bet" for him to say the prayer. I said, "You can't lose."

From time to time I would ask him, "Dad, did you ever say that prayer I asked you to say?"

Most of the time he would just answer, "No. I didn't say that prayer. Tell me the words again." So, I would. At times he got annoyed with me, but once or twice he grinned and said, "Yes, I said the prayer. Is that what you want me to tell you? It isn't true, but if that's what you want to hear, I'll make you happy." Although I would laugh with him, sometimes he caught that little look of sadness in my eyes, and he knew it really meant a lot to me.

One time when I asked him the question, he said, "Yeah, I did say the prayer," then rolling his eyes in feigned ecstasy he added, "and. . .ooooh, ahhhh, ahhh, ooooh. . ."

I immediately said to him, "Stop it, Dad! That's *not* funny! You don't mock God, Dad. He doesn't take it lightly. It's one thing to mess with *my* head, but you don't want to mess with *Him*." Then, in equally feigned humor, I made a fist and laid it against his chest. We both grinned.

One day when I brought up the subject again he really snapped at me, saying, "Why do you keep bothering me with this? Why can't you just let it drop?" He just glared at me, waiting for an answer.

"Because it's too important to me, Daddy. And because I love you, that's why." My answer caught him off guard and his voice softened a little bit.

"Yeah, well, I know that, but you know I just don't believe," he said, shaking his head.

I pressed in. "Can't you just say a little prayer and ask God that if He is real, He will *help* you to believe?" Once more, he just shook his head. For him, it was impossible. He had no foundation, nothing to latch on to. He simply didn't believe.

"I just don't see why you can't let it go," he repeated as he walked away.

I followed him, and once more, I pressed in. "I'll tell you why, Dad. Because *it's* not only important, *you are!* Listen! If you bought a brand new car and the day came for you and Mom to pick it up from the showroom, what would be the first thing you would do after you had driven it around a bit? You *know* what you would do! You would show up at my house and say, 'Come on. Get in. I want to take you for a ride.' You would want to share your good fortune with me, right?" He nodded. "Well, don't you understand, I've found something so wonderful, so much more precious than a new car, something so beyond anything you can even imagine, that I want to share my good fortune with you, too? You see, there's nothing that can compare with having Jesus in your life. . ." My voice trailed off at that point because I was crying.

My father reached out, put his hand on my shoulder, and said softly, "I do understand, Carole, but I'm just not ready."

Although I brought up the subject from time to time, several years passed and nothing seemed to change. However, I kept right on praying for his salvation and never gave up. During that time my father had been fighting a rare form of lymphoma, which is a type of cancer. The time had come when he was in a hospital, dying. Things looked hopeless because he had lapsed into a coma, but I was praying now more than ever. The time was too short.

The day came when the entire family was summoned to the hospital, and we were all at his bedside. I was sitting there saying to God, "God, You have to do something! Please. This is not just my will." I reminded Him of His Word, "Your Word says that it's Your will that *none* should perish. So You can't let him die like this. Please. I've been praying for years and You just have to do *something!*"

I knew my father could hear me even though he was in a coma, and I asked my mother if I could pray with him to accept Jesus.

She adamantly refused, saying, "No, because if he hears you praying he might think he's dying and he'll get frightened."

"He *is* dying!" I answered. "And *you're* the one who's afraid to face that fact. He's going to have a whole lot more to be frightened of, for all eternity for that matter, if he dies in the state he's in now." I was almost frantic to get my mother out of the room, and two of my nieces finally convinced her to go down to the cafeteria for a sandwich. Miraculously, just minutes after they left, my dad opened his eyes for the first time in days. Oh, what a merciful, faithful God we serve!

Those of us still in the room were jubilant to see him suddenly so wide awake and alert, as though there was nothing wrong with him and he had just awakened from a short nap. He greeted us all by name, and after we hugged, kissed, and chatted for a short while, I brought up the old subject again. I said, "Dad, it's time. You're not going to get another chance."

He just looked at me and said, "Yes, it's time." Praise God, when I asked if he was ready to pray with me to accept Jesus, he calmly assented. I pulled the curtain around his bed and, as I prayed, everyone else in the family bowed their heads and repeated the words as well. It was so wonderful to hear my dad praying for the very first time, and when he said the words, "I accept you, Jesus, as my Lord and Savior," his voice broke and he wept. So did we.

But, there's more to the story. When I finished praying with my father, from behind the curtain around his bed I heard a man's voice say, "That was the most beautiful prayer I have ever heard."

I peered around to see one man in the bed and another sitting in a chair next to him. They both had tears in their eyes.

I asked them, "Did you say the prayer with us?"

"No," they answered, "we didn't think we were allowed to."

"Would you like to say it now?" I asked.

Beaming, both of them answered a resounding, "Yes!" So we prayed together and two more names were added to the Lamb's Book of Life. Glory!

We summoned my mother from the cafeteria and she was joyous to see my father awake and alert once more. He remained conscious for three hours, just enough to spend some quality time with my mother, and then he lapsed back into the coma and died two hours later. That's the mercy of God!

It makes me grin to think that when my father got up there, he must have been a-hooting and a-hollering, saying, "It's true! It's real! She was right, there is a heaven." And I get teary to think of how he must have felt to be in the presence of his Savior and feel his Father's love for the very first time.

Who can compare with our God? No one! There is no limit to His mercy and loving-kindness. All those years of praying finally paid off after all. What a faithful, wonderful, loving God He is. Do you have a seemingly hopeless situation? Don't give up. Press in. Keep praying. God is able!

The Almost Divorce

And Jesus looked at them and said, "With man it is impossible, but not with God; all things are possible with God."

—Mark 10:27 (NIV)

I had given my situation a long, hard look. For a change this was one over which I had at least *some* degree of control. Then I made a bold statement, "If I have anything to say about it, and I *do*, this will be done *my way! Nothing will change my mind!*" At least that's what I *thought*. However, God had other ideas.

Rudy and I had been married for over twenty-four years, but they were not years of marital bliss. Not at all. Once more, I see no point in going through all the whys and wherefores of what the problems were. Let me just say that as far as I was concerned, the partnership was over. From early on and throughout most of our marriage, I had sought help from counselors and clergymen, and several times I had been advised to get out of it. However, either because of fear, not wanting to admit failure, or whatever my reasons, I was determined to "hang in there." I have read many books about why people stay in unhealthy relationships, and I was a classic case. In my emotionally damaged state, I kept thinking and hoping it would someday get better. It didn't.

Now things were different. Our daughters were grown and living on their own, and I finally felt I had had enough. Although the Bible told us Jesus had come to give us abundant life, somewhere along the way it seemed to have passed me by. The thought of being alone was frightening, but I felt that anything had to be an improvement over the way I was living. It simply could not go on any longer. This situation must be similar to a person facing major heart surgery. The thought is so scary, you keep putting it off until the time comes when the present pain becomes so intolerable, you are willing to endure an even worse pain because you know it's only temporary. You know that eventually the time will come when you will feel better and be healthier. This is what I wanted.

Several months earlier we had both gone to lawyers, and although we were legally separated, we were still living in the same house. Finances were such that neither of us could afford to pay another rent on top of the mortgage payment and other expenses we had to deal with. To say the least, it was a very awkward situation. Rudy "lived" downstairs in our finished basement, and I "lived" upstairs. I cooked supper for him every night, but we rarely sat or ate together. Anyone who knows me personally knows I can talk on the telephone for twenty minutes to a wrong number. Yet, for over six months Rudy and I said neither hello, nor good-bye, nor anything that was not critical enough to discuss. We acknowledged one another politely when necessary but, except for bills, we shared nothing. Our granddaughter Heather had not yet been born, so there was no joy to be exchanged between us.

About a year earlier, I had left the denominational church I attended for most of my life and was now going to a different church, a "full-gospel" church. That is where I first heard about the prayer of salvation and the need to accept Jesus as my Savior. For the first time I heard the Word of God being taught in a way that made it come alive for me. It was then I began reading and studying the Bible in earnest. In fact, God's pull on my life is what seemed to bring about the chasm that was ever widening between Rudy and me.

In order not to have any possible misunderstanding, in no way am I implying that God caused the rift between us. It is just that for years, aside from what was going on *around* me, I was aware that there was a terrible void in my life, and something was drastically wrong on the inside. It was as though I was slowly starving to death, both in the church I was attending and in my marriage. Now, for the first time in my life, I was being fed and nurtured at the level of my deepest needs. All my life I had been looking for someone else, some other person, to comfort me and ease the pain in my soul. Now I had found Jesus, and He was becoming my Life and my Sustenance.

As the months went by, I continued reading the Bible and was constantly seeking God's will in everything, especially in this issue of the divorce. I knew this is what *I* wanted, but I kept asking God to let me know what *His* will was for me. My dilemma was that no matter where I looked in the Word I could find nothing to justify divorce, except in the case of adultery, and that was not our problem. So, I kept asking, seeking and knocking. From time to time I kept reminding God and tried to convince Him that even *He* knew the way we were living was not a way to live. He did.

Sometimes people use the threat of breaking up as a ploy or manipulation, simply to get the other person to change. This was not the case with me. I had explored every possible avenue and had finally reached a point where I definitely wanted out. After so many years and so many broken promises, I was determined not to be swayed. There were no tears. I had already cried all the tears there were to cry. In fact, at the time I was no longer even angry with Rudy. I felt nothing. Absolutely nothing.

Months went by, and the time came to finalize the divorce papers. During this time of waiting, my source of joy was getting to know Jesus and being part of the Body of Christ. I was so grateful that the church I was attending had weekly Bible studies, as well as other activities which kept me busy. They helped fill some of the emptiness in my life. With each passing day I was growing and learning to trust and love the Lord more and more, and I kept the Thy-will-be-done door open to my heart. I was determined to line up my will with God's will, but I was really hoping that what He wanted was what I wanted, too. I often said to Him, "If You tell me unmistakably that the divorce is not Your will and You want me to stay in this marriage, I won't be happy, Lord, but I'll do it. Then I'll just have to believe You have Your reasons, and I'll have to go along with them." Then I would add, "But please, Jesus, let this thing go through. Please."

It was customary in the church I was attending to have visiting preachers come from time to time to minister to the congregation with either a testimony or a teaching. The church always gave out flyers, and the week before we were going to sign the final divorce papers, I had taken one of those flyers and put it up on the refrigerator with a magnet. On this particular Sunday, the former actress, Lauren Chapin, was coming to our church. As a little girl she was on the *Father Knows Best* television series, the one the father used to call "Kitten." As an adult, she became a heroin addict and spent several years in prison for passing a bad check. That's where Jesus met her, and she gave her life to Him. When she got out, she began going around the country preaching the Word and giving her testimony.

Rudy had always been a movie buff. In fact, at one time we used to joke that he could probably recite the names of every bit actor in the pyramid-building scene of the Ten Commandments. So, when he saw the flyer with Lauren Chapin's name, he recognized it immediately. One night at the dinner table Rudy asked if the Lauren Chapin on the flyer was the same little girl from the television series. When I said she was, he was surprised and asked why she was coming to "*my*" church. I told him she was coming to tell the story of her life and to give her testimony. He showed some surprise but did not respond. We were going to separate churches, and at one time he had sworn he would never come to my church under any circumstances.

The week went by and it was now the Saturday evening before the divorce papers were to be signed on Monday morning. That night I was propped up in bed reading my Bible and talking to God. I was saying, "Well, Lord, it's the eleventh hour. Monday we sign the papers. I can't thank You enough for getting me out of this. But I still need to make sure it's what *You* want for me. I mean, You haven't really answered me. I can't find anything in Your Word that says it's okay. In fact, You say You hate divorce, but I also know You don't want me to continue living this way. So please give me a definitive answer." Just as I was sitting there reasoning with the Lord, Rudy came to the door.

He asked, "What time does the service start in your church tomorrow morning?"

I immediately got defensive and asked him, "Why? Why do you want to know?"

"I thought I might go check it out," he answered. Without even looking at him, I said the service was at eleven o'clock, and he walked away.

At this point, I had a few questions for God. I asked, "Okay, God, what are You doing? Is this the sign I just asked for? Oh, please, let it not be a sign. Not now. Not after all this time. Do You know how many years I have put up with everything? And how many years I prayed for a change? And how long it took me to finally make a decision to get out? And *now* You are making a move? Is this it? Is this part of Your answer? Oh, please tell me it's not!" When the Bible talks about the deceitfulness of the heart, is it ever true. Although I had just finished praying, "Thy will be done," and asking Him to give me a sign, ungrateful little wretch that I was, I was definitely miffed with God.

The next morning I tiptoed around and tried to dress as quietly as possible so as not to let Rudy know I was up. When I got to the kitchen, I was totally annoyed to find that he was already up and dressed. We ate breakfast in silence, and then he announced that he wanted to go to my church. He asked, "Would you want to go with me in my car?"

I was very snippy with him, as I answered, "No thank you. I can get there by myself."

"Oh, come on," he said, "how is it going to look if we both go there in separate cars?"

Now I really snapped back, "Look? Look to whom? They don't even know who you are. And besides, why should you care what my *friends* think of you? You've never cared enough about what *I've* thought of you to make a change, so why should it bother you what *they* think?"

At that point, I was deliberately trying to provoke an argument with him. I wanted to get him angry enough to say, as he had said hundreds of times before in other situations, "Just for that, I'm not going!" It didn't work!

Was this God? It had to be, because instead of getting angry, Rudy quietly asked, "Please, Carole, can we please go together in my car?"

Now I knew for sure it *was* God, and I had to go with the flow. I changed my attitude and the tone of my voice and said, "Yes."

The praise and worship was wonderful, and when Lauren Chapin got up she began preaching the Word of God. She was so filled with the Holy Spirit, and the time went by so swiftly that she never got around to giving her testimony. When she realized how late it was, she apologized and asked Pastor if the congregation could possibly come back that night. He said yes, and the time was fixed for seven o'clock. Before she left she asked if anyone wanted to come up for prayer, and I sat there in total disbelief as Rudy stood up and walked down the aisle. I couldn't even imagine what was going on with him and I was in a state of total bewilderment as to what God was up to. We drove home in silence, each of us deep in our own thoughts.

That afternoon I had been invited to attend the twenty-fifth anniversary party of some very dear friends and I went there alone. Much to my chagrin, Rudy showed up at the same party and came and sat next to me. As the evening wore on, I told my hostess that I had to leave early because there was a service at church I wanted to attend.

With this, Rudy chimed in, "Yes. We have to be at church by seven." Those who knew about our situation lifted questioning eyebrows and I responded in like manner. Who knew *what* was going on? *I* certainly didn't.

You have to understand that on the one hand I wanted God's will for my life, but on the other I wanted out of this marriage, for no other reason than to live my life in peace with the Lord, doing all He wanted me to do. Needless to say, we went to church in the same car, and when the invitation went forth once more for those who needed prayer, Rudy went up a second time. I didn't know it, but this time he gave his heart to Jesus. Oh, God, Your ways are so unsearchable!

Late that night, I was sitting up in bed reading and Rudy came to the door once more. He said, "Let me ask you something. If I were willing to go for counseling, would you be willing to put off signing the papers tomorrow morning? I gave my heart to Jesus tonight, and this time I really want to try to work things out the right way. . .God's way."

The rest is history. Of course, we never signed the papers and with God's help we did work things out. Was it easy? No. Was I ever sorry I changed my mind? Yes. Nevertheless, over a period of time the Lord was able to restore our marriage and even revive my love for him.

In 1989, Rudy went Home to be with the Lord. God had given us five more years together to work out His plan for our lives. During that time, we had the added blessing of being able to share the many joys of having our granddaughter, Heather, become part of our lives.

To my human understanding, nothing could have saved this marriage but God. That's all that was needed. It was He Who spoke to nothing and created something, Who spoke to chaos and created order, Who spoke to darkness and created light. Only He Who called Lazarus out of the deadness of his tomb could have called life out the deadness of this marriage. I thought it was impossible. . .but, with God, all things are possible.

A Year Full of Miracles

Trust in the Lord with all thine heart and lean not on
thine own understanding; in all thy ways acknowledge
Him and He shall direct thy path.
—Proverb 3:5,6

*M*ost people today don't believe in miracles, much
less a whole year full of them. The definition of a
miracle is "an extraordinary happening that mani-
fests God's divine intervention into human affairs." For
those who do believe in miracles, too often they expect some
super spectacular event to occur, when all the while the
miracles are happening every day right under their noses.
The trouble is most of the time they can't be seen unless
one looks with spiritual eyes.

This is how I view the year 1988. It was one of the most
eventful years of my life, and one so full of mini-miracles
that I feel they have to be told so that God will be glorified.
It was during the period of time after our "almost divorce."
Rudy and I were attending church regularly, working hard
at restoring our marriage, and growing in our relationship
with the Lord and with each other. It was a good time.

The year before I had compiled some scriptures from
the Bible, which I used as prayers for my family and myself. I typed them up on a sheet of paper and found it helped
me considerably to read them aloud every day. Then it occurred to me that perhaps other people might also benefit
from reading those particular scriptures. I asked my pastor
for permission to leave some copies on the back table of
the church and he said I could. Week after week, people
kept asking the pastor for more, and within six months I

had put out over five hundred copies. By that time my original copy had gotten so dog-eared, I got the idea that perhaps I should have them made into a booklet.

At the time I was working for a pharmaceutical company, and occasionally we utilized the services of a printer. One day while giving him a printing job, I gave him a copy of the scriptures and asked if he could possibly let me have some ballpark figures about what the cost would be to set the pages up into booklet form. Instead, when he returned the job, he had done them up on a computer and gave them back to me already laid out into eight neat little pages.

When I first saw them I got a knot in the pit of my stomach. I knew how expensive it was to have that kind of work done and I didn't have the money. When the printer saw the look on my face, he just laughed and said, "Don't worry, because there's no charge. My typesetter was really slow the other day, and she was actually glad to have something to do. In fact, she told me it was a long time since she has prayed or even thought about God and this made her do a little thinking."

The wheels began turning in my head and I took it as a go-ahead sign from the Lord. For about a week, I thought about how I had always wanted to do a teaching from chapter six of Ephesians on the "whole armor of God." I wondered what it would cost to add more material to the little booklet and I put the matter before the Lord. As I dialed the printer, I began to pray, "God, if this is of You and not just my wanting to see something of mine in print, would You please give me another sign by making it something I can afford?" At the time I could afford *nothing*, but I knew if God wanted me to do it He would make a way.

The printer's wife answered the telephone and I explained the situation. I asked if she could tell me how much it would cost to make a cover and actually print up some of the eight-page booklets. I could hear the sound of the printing press making a lot of background noise, so she had to raise her voice above the din. She relayed the question to her husband and I heard him yell, "Tell her it depends on how many books she wants printed. Does she want five hundred or a thousand?"

Now I was beginning to have heart palpitations as I said to the woman, "I can't tell you how many books I want printed until I know what the price will be. First I need to know the cost of a hundred books before I can tell you if I want five hundred or a thousand."

Then, in spite of my nervousness, I *really* got bold. "But, before you even ask that question, would you please ask him what it would cost if instead of eight pages, it was sixteen pages?"

Once more she conveyed the message, and all the while I kept praying, "Please, God, if this is of You, please make it something I can somehow afford."

While I was praying I heard the voice of the printer calling back to his wife saying, "Tell her what's the difference? Eight pages, sixteen pages, thirty-two pages, five hundred copies, a thousand copies, what's the difference? It's on the house." I almost fainted. It was a miracle!

His wife said with a resigned tone in her voice, "My husband just lost his mind." Yes! Yes! Yes!

That was how my first book, *Fight the Good Fight*, came into being. It is a book on intercessory prayer and spiritual warfare. The first printing was a blue, thirty-two-page booklet, and we printed two thousand copies. The next was sixty-four pages, and we printed twenty thousand. Many people came to know it simply as the "little blue book," and some actually wrote for it by that name. At the time of this writing there are forty-eight thousand copies of the smaller version of the book in circulation, and there is now a full-sized, expanded edition of the book in print. So, the "little blue book" has grown up.

As a side note, several years ago some missionaries wrote and asked for permission to translate the book into the Tamil language. This is the main language spoken in southern India, and the missionaries are now printing thousands of copies for distribution in that part of India. God works in wondrous ways!

His perfect timing was at work once again. In May I finished the final draft of the book on the very weekend Heather came to live with us permanently. That in itself was another miracle, because since she was born we had been praying for God to do something to get her away from the terrible conditions in which she was living. Jacqueline's condition had reached such a low point that in my heart I had already determined I wasn't going to let her go back. Still, while Rudy and I were ecstatic to have Heather, there were some practical and legal issues that needed to be worked out.

I was still working a full time job, which created a problem. Heather was six months short of the age she needed to be before she could go into a daycare center. My employers knew my situation and were very sympathetic. I couldn't afford a full-time baby sitter, so occasionally my department head allowed me to take her to work with me. One of the warehouse workers brought in some huge, brand new boxes, and we set up a play area in a corner of the office. Heather was so well behaved that she would play quietly for hours. Everyone loved her. Many of my coworkers would come and visit her on their breaks, bringing her toys and all kinds of goodies, much to her delight. God worked it all out. A few days a week my husband took her with him to his real estate job, and on the other days we had some friends from our church that took care of her.

A Year Full of Miracles

One Friday night after intercessory prayer at church, I was introduced to a young man named Mark. Another miracle was on its way. I was holding Heather in my arms, and he commented on what a pretty little girl she was.

He asked, "Is she yours?"

"No," I said, smiling. "She's my granddaughter. I wish she *was* mine. In fact, my husband and I have had her for several months now, and although we've been trying, we haven't been able to get even get temporary custody. Aside from the fact that we want her, without legal custody or guardianship, doctors or hospitals will refuse to even treat any child if you are not the actual parents. That means if she ever gets sick, we don't even have the authority to get medical attention for her. It's very upsetting."

His eyes showed deep concern as he listened. I continued, "Our problem is that money is very tight and custody cases are very expensive. I've called several lawyers to try and get legal custody of her, but we just can't afford their fees." We talked some more, and then he gave both Heather and me a reassuring hug before we parted.

On Sunday morning after service, the same young man walked over to me with a big smile on his face as he handed me a business card. He said, "I was talking to a lawyer friend of mine about your situation, and he is willing to take this case without charge. Call him this week for an appointment." I was so overwhelmed that I didn't even know what to say. We hugged once more, and Rudy and I left there rejoicing at what was taking place. Only God's provision could have done something so incredible.

Later that week we found out from the lawyer that Mark had agreed to pay all the legal fees connected with Heather's custody case. However, the lawyer said that although he would not charge us anything for handling the case itself, it would take at least five or six days in court for us to even get temporary custody and many more days after that to get permanent custody. He felt that would be too great a financial burden for his friend. He said we would have to pay the fee for those days ourselves. Once more, Rudy and I trusted in God and somehow we knew He would provide.

At the time I was fifty-two years old and it was becoming increasingly exhausting to work a full-time job, run a house, and be mommy at night. I thought that was causing the incredible fatigue and abdominal pains I had been feeling for some time. When I finally went to a doctor, it turned out that I had a serious medical problem. By July, I was diagnosed as having a large mass in my abdominal cavity, and in August I underwent major surgery.

The surgeon removed a seven-pound sarcoma that had grown around a portion of my small intestines and around part of the colon. Praise God, the cancer was removed intact, along with several feet of intestines. It was diagnosed as a liomyosarcoma, a type of cancer for which they have never had a single remission from using either chemotherapy or radiation. Consequently, none was offered. The surgeon felt he had gotten it all and, because it was "contained," I was given a clean bill of health. Glory!

God made good use of my twenty-one-day hospital stay, because during that time I prayed with eleven people who received Jesus as their Savior. Needless to say, after I went home, there was a lot of residual pain and recuperation was slow. Once more, God worked it out. Somehow, between my husband, our friends, and whatever little I could do, we all got by.

It turned out that the court hearing for Heather's custody was exactly one month from the date of my surgery. I was determined to be there even if I had to crawl into court, but I didn't have to. I kept repeating Philippians 4:13, which says I could do all things through Christ Who strengthens me—and He did! Who else but God could have orchestrated the events of that day in the way they worked out?

The case was supposed to have been heard at nine o'clock in the morning, but instead, we sat in the waiting area until it was ten minutes before the court convened for lunch. We were so discouraged because the hour was late and our lawyer had to leave soon. We didn't think anything would be accomplished at all that day, but finally we heard our names being called. When we got into the courtroom our attorney quickly presented the case and all the documents. The judge listened, then looked over all the information we had compiled and abruptly announced, "I see no reason why these grandparents should be given temporary custody of this child." At this my heart sank. Then he continued, "I see no reason why they should not be given permanent custody. Permanent custody granted!" With that he hit the gavel on the desk and said, "I'm going to lunch."

Our lawyer turned to us and said, "You just got yourselves a miracle. And I'm going to give you a second one. I'm not charging you anything for today." Hallelujah! The miracles were beginning to add up.

When I look back on all that transpired, I realize one of God's very important principles was at work. It has to do with obedience in tithing and giving to others. I can remember having a conversation with my mother during a period in our lives when our finances were at an extremely low point. She had said, "I hope you're not still giving all that money to your church, Carole, because frankly, you can't afford it."

I just looked at her and responded, "Frankly, Mom, I can't afford not to. God has promised that if we are faithful to Him in the matter of tithing, He will be faithful to us beyond what we could ever imagine. I've found out, Mom, that you cannot 'outgive' God." She just frowned and shook her head.

One year, that's all it was, but what enormous changes took place in our lives in such a small period of time. I am staggered by the mountain of miracles. Over and over again God proved Himself faithful. He brought me through a potentially deadly infirmity with a clean bill of health. He allowed me to write *Fight the Good Fight* and arranged for it to be printed. He also continued to meet all of our financial needs through many different circumstances. More importantly, Heather was delivered out of the terrible situation in which she was living, and we got permanent custody.

I know that none of these are the kind of miracles that make headlines. They weren't meant to. However, in the story of my life they stand out in big letters. The dictionary meaning of miracles doesn't even come close to describing how I feel about God's divine intervention in our lives. He brought me to a place of trust in Him that I never thought was possible. Won't you please join me in praising Him and saying "We serve a mighty God."

Learning to Trust

Trust in the Lord and do good; so shalt thou dwell in the land, and verily thou shalt be fed. Commit thy way unto the Lord; trust also in Him; and He shall bring it to pass.
—Psalm 37:3, 5

I looked down at the check in my hand. It was for several thousand dollars. "Okay," I asked, grinning at Rudy, "now are you going to tell me where all this money came from?"

His face got very serious as he said, "I cash-surrendered my life insurance policy." I felt my stomach turn, but there was nothing I could do about it. It was already done and couldn't be undone.

It was June, 1989, just ten months after my first bout with cancer. I was still feeling a lot of residual pain from the surgery, but I had resumed all my duties and was back working full time because money was tight.

As I mentioned earlier, the course of events of the past year had taken its toll emotionally on Rudy. Heather was the only real ray of sunshine in his inner storm, but for several weeks now, he had not been feeling well physically. Although he was under a doctor's care and being treated for a respiratory problem, I suspected something else was seriously wrong with him. Despite all the medications, not only was he not getting any better, he was getting worse with each passing day. Needless to say, circumstances were very difficult.

Thank God for Heather, because she was then three-and-a-half years old, a total delight, and the highlight of our lives. In a word, she was "delicious." She was living with us for over a year, but every night when I went to pick her up at the daycare center, I still felt a surge of joy at the prospect of seeing her beautiful little face.

Rudy and I were managing, but financially things were very rough and the bills were piling up. Earlier in the week he had told me he was expecting a check to come in but he wouldn't say from where. This really puzzled me. I knew it wasn't from any commission, because he hadn't had a sale from his real estate job in a very long time. Sure enough, on that Thursday the sorely needed check had come in the mail. So here we were on Saturday afternoon writing out check after check, until all the money was gone except for three hundred dollars.

When he told me he had cash-surrendered his insurance policy, there were so many things I wanted to say. As I quickly turned them over one by one in my mind, they all sounded so selfish that I decided they were better left unsaid. I thought of how many rough situations the Lord had already brought us through, and I comforted myself with the assurance that He would work this out for us as well.

"You'd better stick around for a while, Mister," I said.

He laughed and answered, "Don't worry. I promised you sixty years when I asked you to marry me, didn't I? And we still have thirty to go." Our eyes held each other's for a moment as we shared the unspoken commitment and decision to love, no matter what.

The following Monday afternoon at work, I had just gotten off the phone from talking with Rudy when the telephone rang again. It was a woman who worked in his office. "Carole," she screamed, "get over to South Nassau emergency room right away. It's Rudy. He's. . .he's. . .just get over there quickly."

In my heart I guess I already knew, because I asked her, "Please, tell me, is he dead?"

"I don't know," she said, "just go!"

I prayed all the way to the hospital and got there within minutes. When I approached the emergency desk and gave his name they said they were working on him but they had no information for me. If you've ever been in that kind of a situation, you know what hospital "run-around" is like. I was pacing back and forth in the emergency room and just kept calling on Jesus, asking Him to help me. I cried and begged the hospital staff to let me see him for a moment, or at least to let me know whether or not he was alive.

Without giving me any information, they led me into a small room apart from the general waiting area. There I was, alone. I whispered a prayer to God, "Please, God, please. . .help him. Please keep him alive. He's only fifty-five. Please give him another chance. Be with him, Lord. He needs You. I do, too, but right now he needs You more. And, Lord, I need *him*. Please, Lord, have mercy."

All the horror of his suffering the night before and that morning flashed through my mind. Deathly pale, he had spent most of the night struggling for breath and sweating profusely. The only way he seemed to be able to breathe was to sit with his chair moved far back from the kitchen table, leaning forward against the edge. I had spent the night either praying, arguing with him to go to the hospital, or crying. Stubborn to the very end, he had refused to go.

Early that morning I reached a point where I said to him, "Rudy, if you don't go willingly to the hospital, I'm going to call an ambulance and have them take you away." He looked at me almost menacingly and said, "If you do, Carole, that will be one of the last things you *ever* do. Do me a favor, will you? Just take Heather to daycare and go to work. Will you do me that favor, please?" I decided that rather than stay at home and argue with him, I would do as he wished. I dressed Heather and left him leaning against the table, gasping for breath.

When I got to work, I spent most of the morning arguing with him back and forth on the telephone. I was nagging him to get to the doctor and threatening to call the ambulance. He was gasping for breath, asserting his place as head of the family, and refusing to go.

In my mind I replayed the last phone conversation I had with him only minutes before his co-worker called me. Somehow he had showered, dressed, and driven to his office, but the strain of all that activity had probably been too much. When he called he had said, "Carole? I just called to say you were right."

That was not something I heard too often, so I questioned him, "Right about what?"

He said, "I'm going to the hospital as soon as I hang up. I just called to say 'don't wait dinner for me, I'll be a little late.' Please kiss Heather for me."

"You really *are* sick, aren't you?" I asked.

"Yes, I think I really am." Overriding his objections, I told him I would leave work and meet him at the hospital, but he interrupted me and said, "Carole. . .?"

"Yes?"

"I just want you to know I love you. Even though you're a real pain sometimes, I want you to know I love you."

"I love you, too, Rudy. . ." I answered.

Once more he interrupted me and said, "But I love Jesus even more." It turned out those were the last words he ever spoke.

Later I found out that just as he hung up the phone, he suffered a fatal, massive heart attack and dropped to the floor. The only reason he was taken to the hospital was because an off-duty policeman and a fireman happened to be in the real estate office at the time, and they had immediately begun doing CPR on him. When the ambulance came, the paramedics had gotten his heart beating again and now the hospital staff was struggling to keep him alive.

My thoughts were interrupted by a soft-spoken nurse who came in and asked if I needed anything. She was thoroughly professional, yet compassionate. I detected a look of sadness in her eyes as she handed me his wallet and then his wedding band. She said, "Here. Put the ring away in a safe place and try not to forget where you put it."

"What are you telling me?" I asked her. "Is he dead?"

She said, "We're doing all we can. I can't tell you anything yet," and she walked out. Somehow, deep inside of me, I knew he was gone.

I stood there alone in that room and looked up toward the ceiling. That's not where God is, I know, but it was my way of sending my words in His direction. "God. . . what. . .? Is he dead? Is he? Did You take him Home? Did You? Oh God, what could You be thinking about? I mean, he's still young. I need him. Heather needs him. And I'm not strong enough. I need him around to help me. I can't do it alone. . .We have no money. . .and there's no insurance. What am I going to do? How are we going to make it. . .?" I was still looking up as my voice trailed off.

Sometimes an odd thing happens when I'm faced with a difficult situation. My mind suddenly begins to examine the circumstances from a different angle. Like so many times before, my thoughts now took an abrupt turn. I suddenly remembered that God already knew all about it. So, out loud, I said to Him, "Wait a minute, God. What? I'm telling *You?* You don't know what's going on? You don't know what I need? You, Who created the heaven and the earth and sustain all things by the word of Your power, You don't *know?* Of course You do! You know it all!" A sob began to rise in my throat as I continued, "Then that means You're going to see me through this. And You have to because *You promised!*"

By this time, I was crying like a little child. "You promised to never leave us nor forsake us. Then that means You're going to see Heather and me through this. Oh God, You have to! That is, *please*, You have to. I mean, if You don't help me, there's no one else who will. Lord will You be there for me? Will You?"

Deep within my inner spirit, I felt His peace flooding into my soul. Now I began weeping in a different way. I told Him, "Okay. It's all right, God. Let Thy will be done. Whatever You want. I know You'll take care of us. I put my trust in You, Lord. There's no other way."

When I look back, I realize that this was the very place to which Jesus wanted me to come. Me, self-sufficient, I-can-do-it-myself, me. I had finally come to the place where I realized my total dependency on Him. I know now that if the circumstances had not been so seemingly hopeless, I would have tried to work it out in my own strength. If I had, I never would have gotten to the point of ever knowing the real power of God in my life, not just in theory, but experientially.

In the weeks immediately following Rudy's death, the number of situations demanding my attention was staggering. There was a mountain of paperwork, bills of every kind were piled high, water pipes broke, money was scarce, Heather was needy, and I felt overwhelmed. What got me through was that every time I thought about some area of my life that I knew I just couldn't handle alone, I forced myself to take my eyes off the circumstance and focus them on the glory and the majesty of Jesus. I would simply start praising God. The result was that He came through—every time!

In the area of finances, my church took up a collection and the entire funeral was paid for. People, even ones I didn't know, sent money from just about everywhere. What's more, outstanding loans were miraculously wiped off computers and somehow marked "Paid." Through all those weeks and months, God continued to give us favor with Him and with people, and He met our needs over and above everything we could have ever hoped or dreamed.

The Bible says that God's grace is sufficient. In fact, one of His names is "El Shaddai, the All-Sufficient-One." That means He is more than enough for any and every situation. It is one thing to know something in theory, but during those months I found that whenever and wherever I was weak, God filled in the gap and His strength found its sufficiency in my weakness. Was I scared? Sometimes. Was I ever overwhelmed and discouraged? Yes. Yet somehow, deep inside I knew He would make a way and show me He is more than able to handle anything I cannot handle. What a comforting thought that was, and still is.

Sometimes I wonder why it takes us so long to "get with the program." How I wish I had learned that lesson sooner in life. What a mountain of worry and strife I could have saved myself. Much as I would never want to have to repeat it, what a great lesson this was in learning to trust.

Have you come to this understanding yet? It's never too late in life to learn it. Are you walking through a valley? God is right there, walking you through it all. Are you in a pit? God knows the address of your pit, and He will pull you out when the time is right. What He did for me He can, and will, do for you. Trust Him. He really cares.

11

A New Family

A father to the fatherless and a judge and protector of
the widow is God in His holy habitation. God places the
solitary in families. . .
—Psalm 68:5,6 (AMP)

*G*randma, who is going to be our daddy now?" Heather
asked.

My mind was racing for an answer as I inwardly
turned to God. "Oh, Lord," I asked Him, "what do I tell
her?" With an assurance in my voice that I wasn't feeling in
my heart, I said, "The Lord. He'll be our daddy from now
on."

That's what my mouth said, but at the time, I was dealing with my own pain and doubts. Even *I* didn't believe
what I was saying, and inwardly I groaned and asked Him,
"God, how is this little child ever going to believe *that?*" I
didn't think she could.

To my surprise, and with the faith only a child can have,
Heather's face brightened and she asked, "He *will*,
Grandma?"

I looked up hopefully and in my heart I asked Him,
"You *will*, Lord?" Deep inside He answered me with an in-
flooding of His peace. More confident now, I said, "Yes,
Heather, He will. He will be our daddy from now on. Do
you know there's a scripture about that? It's in Psalm 68.
Hurry and get the Bible and we'll read it together."

I understand why Jesus said we have to come to Him as
little children. They *believe!* While she ran to get the Bible,
my mind began to analyze what was going on inside of me.
It was not as though I didn't *trust* God, but there were so

many things to do, so many adjustments to be made. The pressure was staggering, and I was weary.

Heather's question let me know that she was having her own share of inner fears. Although she didn't know how to verbalize them, somehow she felt detached from all the wonderful connotations that the word *family* had meant to her. Rudy's death had left her feeling abandoned and incomplete. Together, the three of us had been a family, and she was not only missing his presence, but the feelings of wholeness and belonging were no longer there. As a result of reading several books on the subject, I learned this is not unusual. It is very common for survivors to feel broken, fragmented, and disconnected. This is especially true for children. Although I tried, it was difficult to consistently "be there" for Heather in her need, because sometimes I felt I wasn't even "there" for myself.

The word *family* has immense meaning for so many people who either do or do not belong to one. The key is *belonging*. Whether a family is a good one or not is beside the point. There is a common bond that lets you feel that at least you're *part* of something.

By now, Heather had returned with the Bible. The two of us sat down and she traced the words with her little finger as I read to her. "It says that He will be a Father to the fatherless and a protector of the widow," I said. "That's you and me, Heather."

She smiled and snuggled into me. "There's even another one in the book of Romans that tells us we have been given a spirit of adoption and we can call God 'Abba.' That means 'daddy' in Hebrew. See? He is your Daddy." At that, she smiled from ear to ear, and her heart was at rest.

We sat quietly for a long time letting the peace of those words sink into our inner spirit. Suddenly Heather sat up with a start and said excitedly, "Grandma, you know what?

I was just thinking. If God is my Father, then that makes me a *princess*, because *He's the King!*"

Once more a smile of joy spread across her face and mine as well, as I thanked and praised Him for His love. Inside, however, I prayed, "God, we need help. We need a family, a new one. You can do it. Please do it, Lord."

Over the years, there were several young people from our church with whom Rudy and I had gotten friendly. At that time, they were all in their thirties and early forties and unattached, and this gave them the freedom to visit with Heather and me whenever they wanted to. What was wonderful was that they *wanted* to. It turned out they were God's answer to my prayer.

On weekends, and especially every Sunday after church, they would all come to our house. They loved to eat and I loved to cook, so it worked out very well for everybody. We spent the day watching Christian tapes or movies, discussing the Bible, playing Bible trivia games, or just "vegging," and enjoying one another's company. We spent lots of good, quality time together, and even shared our summer vacations. Those were glorious days of experiencing God's beauty, bounty, and love. During the first few years when Heather was most needy, one very special young man named David became a wonderful father figure for her. Whether we were hiking across meadows, walking through the woods, or at the beach, he would often take her hand or carry her on his shoulders. He helped fill the void and ease the pain of her loss.

Each year on my birthday or Mother's Day, my new family bought me flowers and took Heather and me out to dinner. Some of them still do. They send cards, and several of them are special "To-my-Mother" cards. I'm so blessed that this is how they think of me, because I also think of them as my children. Although some of them now have families of their own, we still see each other often, and over the years our love and respect have continued to grow.

As long as we are alive, circumstances will continue to test our faith. Each time another test comes along, I look back at what God has already done and I am comforted. It reminds me of the hymn that talks about God's great faithfulness to us and how His hand has provided our every need. It is so true! I also love how the Bible tells us about the extraordinary, selfless love the Father has given to us, enabling us to be called the children of God. What a comfort it is to know that He is our Father, and we are a part of *His* family.

I Live in His Heart

Blessed *are* the pure in heart for they shall see God.
—Matthew 5:8

*H*eather, get away from that window and come over here," I said, almost in desperation. "I can't stand seeing you there any more."

She turned and said to me, "But Grandma, you don't understand. Every night when I say my prayers I ask Jesus if He would 'pleeease' let lovey Grampy come down from heaven for a teensie, weensie little bit. Just so I could sit on his lap for a little while. Then he can go back to heaven. And I'm waiting, Grandma. Maybe he'll come tonight!"

I couldn't take it any more. Every evening for the past three weeks I watched her keep vigil at the living room window, waiting to see his car pull into the driveway. It was bad enough having to deal with my own pain, but to watch Heather grieving so badly over the loss of her grandfather was almost more than I could bare. It tugged at that inner part of me that always wants to rescue other people. Somehow, it is easier to deal with someone else's pain than to have to deal with your own. It was one of those times when the boundaries between us were blurred and I no longer knew where her anguish ended and mine began. Worse than that, I didn't know what to do to help her. All I could do was pray.

For the past year we had developed a regular procedure. Each night while I was preparing supper, Rudy used to take Heather downstairs to the basement and they would either pound on the upright piano together or she would snuggle with him in the big, overstuffed chair while they watched television. Everything had changed since his death, and Heather's behavior reflected that change. Now she wouldn't even walk down the stairs with me when I went to do laundry, and she didn't want to even look at the piano.

On this particular night, I felt I could no longer bear the pain. I put on a Christian videotape for her to watch and went into my bedroom, sank down to my knees, and wept. I prayed fervently to Jesus and cried out to Him, "Please, Jesus, do something special just for her. She's had so much loss in her little life. Please let her know how much You love her. My love doesn't seem to be enough for her right now. She needs You. I don't know how You can do it, but I know You can. Please, in some very real way let her know that You will be the father she has never known. Fill that need for her and ease the pain of losing her Grandpa." I remained there for some time weeping and praying until she came to find me.

Bedtime was always a happy time for us and we both looked forward to the routine we had developed. I would lie next to her on the bed, and after we said our prayers, we would sing songs to the Lord until she fell asleep. That night we were on the second time around of singing a song that tells the Lord how much we love and adore Him. Heather was singing to Jesus with all her heart, "Jesus, I adore You, lay my life be-e-fore You, how I lu-uv. . ." All of a sudden, without even finishing the line, she stopped singing. Her voice didn't fade or trail off, but it came to an abrupt stop. I was lying there and thought, *Oh, how cute! She fell asleep right in the middle of the song, right in the middle of the line. How sweet. . .*I stayed there for about ten minutes longer while my mind wandered off somewhere.

Suddenly, Heather whispered softly to me, "Grandma?"

Startled, I answered, "Oh, Heather. I thought you were asleep. Have you been awake all this time?"

"Grandma," she repeated, "do you know what? Jesus just came to me." In her sweet, still-little-baby talk, she continued, "And you know what He *tolded* me? He *tolded* me He *loves* me. And you know what else? He *holded* me in His arms very close to His chest and I could hear His heart beating. And you know what? He *tolded* me I live in His heart."

I didn't know how to respond. At this point my own heart was pounding. "He *did*?" I asked. "He was *here*?" I just lay there stunned for an instant. I thought, *Jesus was here? She saw Him? And He told her she lives in His heart?* My mind was racing and I felt almost giddy.

She continued, "Yes, Grandma. He was right here."

Like the playback of a tape, my mind kept reviewing what she said. I find it humorous that even at a time like that the "writer and editor" part of my brain took over. Mentally I began to rearrange her words. I thought, *She said Jesus told her she lives in His heart, but she must have misunderstood. She must mean He said He lives in her heart.* So, I said back to her, "You mean Jesus told you He lives in *your* heart?"

"No, Grandma," she answered, "He said I live in *His* heart."

Stunned, I thought, *Praise God, she couldn't be making this up. He really was here and He really did speak to her. That's just what He told her! He said she lives in His heart.*

My mind was reeling and I could barely take it in. This was not some Christian trying to impress another Christian with their beatific vision. This was just a little three-and-a-half-year-old child who didn't know that seeing Jesus was not an everyday experience. Praise began pouring out from my heart to God for His kindness, mercy, and love.

My mind was spinning at the thought that while I was there next to her, the Lord Jesus Christ was also there, holding her and talking with her.

Suddenly the awe and reverence left me and my humanness took over. I said to Him, "And what am I, chopped liver? What about me? I mean, I didn't even get goose bumps! Not even one! You, the Lord Jesus Christ, Creator of the entire universe, were here just now. And I was right here. And I didn't feel a *thing!* How come?" I whined. "How come *I* didn't see You, too? I mean, how about doing something special for the grandmother, huh? After all, I'm the one who said the prayer. Don't You know I need something, too?" What selfish, greedy little piggies we humans are, never satisfied with anything! For the moment, in my self-centered blindness, I couldn't see that He *had* done something special for me. He answered my prayer for Heather better than I could ever have imagined.

Slowly the understanding came to me as to why she had seen Him and I had not. It was obvious. The Scripture says, "Blessed are the *pure in heart*, for *they* shall see God." (Matthew 5:4) (Italics mine.) I can only dimly imagine His delight in hearing a little child with a pure heart singing a song of love to Him. Is it any wonder that He came to Heather and let her see Him?

Finally, the full realization of what happened began to gel in my mind. The Lord had given me one more wonderful experience to be able to look back on for reassurance when I needed it. He showed me that without a doubt, He not only hears every prayer, but He is a prayer-answering God. He really *is* with us. Although we mortals are always looking for the spectacular, every once in a while He takes an ordinary moment in an ordinary person's life and graces it with His presence. What could be more spectacular than that?

For several days after that incident, Heather had a visible glow about her and a continuous smile on her face. We were able to bask in the memory of the visitation for quite some time, and it carried both of us over the many storms that were to follow. Unfortunately, as she got older she was no longer able to recall the experience to her conscious memory. Whenever I tell the story, she feels a touch of sadness because she can only enter into the wonder of the experience as a listener. Nevertheless, she knows it really *did* happen.

In recent years, there have been times when Heather has been hurt by the opinions and actions of some of her peers. Sometimes she cries because she feels she "just doesn't belong." When that happens, I say to her, "Welcome to the club, Heather. We *don't* belong. We *are* different. *You* are different, Heather." I remind her of that night when Jesus actually held her and told her she lives in His heart. Then I add, "Remember that there are not too many people in the world who have actually heard the heart of God. But you did. I have no idea why He gave you that wonderful visitation, but you can be sure He had His good reason for it. You'll see. Someday He'll bring it back to you and use it for His very special purpose in your life." She smiles, and it sustains and helps carry her through.

Have you ever wondered what our lives would be like if only we had the innocence and purity of a little child? Maybe we would be able to look around us in all the wonder and joy that we lost as we gained what the world calls "sophistication." If only we could *truly* be pure in heart, then maybe we would be able to see the many times God touches our lives in a special way and we're never the same. Then maybe, just like angels and little children, we too might see Him face to face.

Angels at the Window

. . .some have entertained angels without knowing it.
—Hebrews 13:2 (NIV)

*T*he thick, black night covered us like a blanket, and the hot, humid air made breathing difficult. Our sleep was suddenly broken by a brilliant flash of light, followed immediately by an earth-shaking clap of thunder that seemed to explode directly over our heads. Flash after flash of lightning crackled and snapped around the house, while roar after roar of thunder reverberated and rolled across the heavens.

I was sharing Heather's bedroom at the time, and in one leap, without ever touching the floor, she was in my bed. "It's all right," I reassured her, "it's very loud, I know, but it's only a thunderstorm." My voice was steady and calm, but inside my own heart skipped a beat with every clap of thunder that exploded around us.

This was the first time I was experiencing what every widowed or single parent must feel when they are facing full responsibility for the safety of a small child. Everything is on your shoulders. Only when people have gone through the experience themselves can they understand what a difference it makes to not have someone else around. It must have been the Holy Spirit reminding me of the reality of Jesus, because as I lay there holding Heather, I suddenly realized we were *not* alone. The storm continued to rage, but knowing He was there changed the whole situation around.

Although it was stifling, Heather was so close to me it felt as though she would come through the other side.

Every inch of her little body was against my side, as if by some kind of osmosis she was trying to absorb as much strength from me as she could. As the thunder continued crashing over our heads she cried out, "Grandma, why does it keep *doing* that?"

Cradling her little head and pulling her even closer, I said, "That's God showing His power in the heavens, Heather. He is all powerful in the universe and there's nothing for us to be afraid of." I paused. "Do you know that there's a song about that? It's a praise song to God. We can sing it sometime. Better still, why don't we sing it to Him right now, Heather."

"*Now*, Grandma?" she asked. "You want to start singing *now*? In the middle of a *storm*?"

"There's no better time," I said. So, we did. We lay there side by side in the bed, and I began to sing:

Oh Lord, my God. When I in awesome wonder,
Consider all of the worlds Thy hands have made.
I see the stars; I hear the rolling thunder,
Thy power throughout the universe displayed.
Then sings my soul, my Savior God, to Thee.
How great Thou art. How great Thou art.
Then sings my soul, my Savior God to Thee.
How great Thou art. How great Thou art.

Heather joined in as our voices blended with the beautiful words of the song and floated out upon the night air. We sang it through several times, and with each chorus of *How Great Thou Art*, her fear slowly ebbed away. Although in the natural the storm still raged on around us, we were engulfed by a peace that could only have come from God. I lay there thinking about the incredible majesty of the Lord and His wonderful faithfulness to us and tears of joy streamed down both sides of my face.

Heather's little voice broke the reverie as she exclaimed with a note of wonder and joy, "Oh Grandma, look! The angels have been singing with us, too. I guess they wanted to come in out of the rain."

"What angels?" I asked, looking around.

She said, "All the angels here in the room with us. Can't you see them? Oh, Grandma, they're *sooooo* big! Almost up to the ceiling! And look, there are two more angels at the window looking in. I guess they heard their friends singing and they came to sing, too." Her face was beaming, and once more the tears rolled.

When I think about that supernatural visitation, I wonder if it really was so supernatural after all. I don't think so. I believe there are such wondrous things that go on around us all the time, but most of us are not privileged to see them. To us they seem to be extraordinary, but to God they are just "business as usual." There must be countless times He sends His angels to surround and protect us, but we are simply not aware of their presence. I never saw the angels that night, but I'm sure they were there to join in our praise and adoration.

I thought about how Psalm 91 tells us that no evil shall befall us, and we need not be afraid of the terror by night because He has given His angels charge over us. These are not just empty words. They are comfort and truth!

Waiting on God

But they that wait upon the Lord shall renew their
strength. . .

—Isaiah 40:31

*I*hate waiting - for *anyone* or *anything*. How about you?
In fact, the most severe testing of my patience comes
from having to wait. In our Christian walk, I would
venture to guess that one of the most difficult kinds of waiting is waiting on God. It doesn't matter if you're young or
old or how long you've been walking the walk, it's still difficult. Whenever I've been praying hard for something and
the answer is slow in coming, I have to keep reminding
myself, "Remember, Carole, God *is* a prayer-answering God.
This is only a test." Then I have to draw on all the times He
has absolutely proven His love and faithfulness.

One thing I do know is that every time I pray, He really
does hear me. Although I may not see the answer or it's not
coming the way I want it to come, in His own inimitable
way, He *is* responding. The problem is, sometimes He answers "yes," sometimes He says "no," sometimes He says
"wait," and *sometimes,* He says, "My grace is sufficient." I
don't like that one, because it always involves pain.

I can still remember a particular lesson Heather and I
learned when Jacqueline was still alive and we were going
through the difficult task of waiting on God. For several
years we had been praying for a miracle that her mother
would be healed in her spirit, soul, and body, enabling her
to leave the life of drugs behind and take her rightful place
of being a mother to this child.

One night as we were preparing for bed, I had just called Heather in to give her some medicine that she had been taking for a bad cough. After she took it, we went into the bedroom and began our prayers. Every night we lifted up the petition about her mother to the Lord, but on this particular night, she stopped me.

"You know, Grandma," she said, "I'm angry at the Lord." I didn't try to argue with her statement, and neither did I decide to give her a sermon. Child or not, like anyone else, she was entitled to her feelings.

Instead, I just asked, "Why, Heather?"

"Well, every night we say prayers for my mommy to be healed and nothing ever happens. God hasn't answered our prayers and I'm angry."

"Oh, but He has," I responded.

"He *has*, Grandma? What do you mean, 'He's answered our prayers.'? Mommy still isn't better. I don't understand."

Turning my heart to the Holy Spirit, I quickly said a silent prayer for wisdom. Actually, what I said to Him was, "Help!"

Aloud, I said, "Well, let me explain it to you. Do you know that every time we say a prayer, God *immediately* sets Himself to answer that prayer? Every time you say a prayer for your mommy the Lord says, "Ah, there's My precious little Heather praying for her mommy. Let Me answer that prayer right away. Then, in the spirit, He calls to her and says, 'Jacqueline, come. Your precious Heather is praying for you to be healed. Come, let Me heal you.'"

I paused for a moment. "Now, do you remember what you did just a little while ago, when I called you in to take your cough medicine? You came in, I poured it on a spoon, you opened your mouth, and you swallowed it. Well, the kind of medicine your mommy needs doesn't come on a spoon, but when the Lord calls her to take her medicine, in the spirit she looks at Him and says, 'Nope!' So you see, it's not that the Lord hasn't answered your prayers, it's that your mommy isn't ready to be healed."

I saw that too familiar tremor begin in her bottom lip as the tears welled up in her eyes. She looked at me with her big brown eyes and said, "But I still want to see her, Grandma."

"I want to see her, too, Heather, but we can't"

Her anger resurfaced and she retorted, "Why not?"

I said, "I know it's what you really want, Heather. And I also know that you're even a little angry at me, because you think I'm the one to blame for your not being able to see her." She nodded. "But as part of my answer let me tell you a true story."

I continued, "Years ago I used to have a beautiful little turquoise parakeet named Percy. He was allowed to fly all around the house anytime he wanted, except when I was cooking dinner or if anyone was about to open a door. He was a very cute, very bright, and very spoiled little bird, and he didn't like being put in his cage even for a moment. He only stayed in there at night when he went to sleep. Whenever I made him go in his cage, he would squawk and screech and pull on the little door trying to get out." I paused. She smiled.

"One night I had put him in because I was starting to make supper. He went into his little tantrum and I said to him, 'I know, I know. You're angry with me because I won't let you out of the cage. But that's because you have a little bird brain. You can't see the danger involved. But I'm a person and much bigger than you and I can see on a much wider scale. I know that if I let you out of your cage, you might be burned by the steam. But you can't see that. So, I'd rather you be angry at me now than if I let you have your way and you might be hurt terribly or might even die."

As Heather listened, I could tell that she was beginning to grasp the meaning of the story. I continued, "Suddenly, while I was talking to Percy, I realized that this is what God says to us sometimes. Sometimes He has to hold something back from us that we want, just so that we won't be hurt. That's because He can see the danger and we can't."

She looked at me and asked, "You mean that's like me seeing my mommy?"

I held her close to me and said, "Yes, Heather, it's *just* like you seeing your mommy. I know the Lord is saying to you right now, 'My precious little Heather. How I long to give you the desires of your heart. But you see, you are only a little girl and you can't see the dangers. I'm God. I can see on a much wider scale. I know if I let you have what you want now, you might be so hurt and so wounded that it will take a long time to get over it. You've had to trust Me so many times already, so won't you please trust Me one more time?'

She lifted her tear-streaked little face to mine as I asked her, "Will you do that, Heather? Will you do that for God and for me? Will you trust Him just one more time? And will you trust *me* once more, too, Heather? Because you know I pray for wisdom every day, and I have to believe that I'm being led by the Lord. What you think *I'm* keeping from you is actually the Lord's way of protecting you. Hasn't He taken good care of us so far?"

She nodded. "He's our Father and He loves us. If God lets us down now, it will be the very first time." She snuggled a little closer into me and we just sat quietly for a time.

A scripture began floating through my mind and I broke the silence between us. "Do you know what we have to do now? The only thing we can do—and that's to keep on praying and waiting upon the Lord."

"What's that, Grandma? What's 'waiting upon the Lord'?"

"It's in the Bible, Heather." I said. And I could see her perking up as her curiosity was roused. She loved whenever I told her there was a Bible scripture that applied to something we were going through. I explained, "There's a scripture in the book of Isaiah about waiting for God to do something for us. God said that whoever waits on Him, while they're waiting, He will strengthen them and do other wonderful things for them."

"What's He doing for us, Grandma?" she asked.

"Well, for one thing He's teaching us to be patient," I answered. "Then He's also teaching us how to become strong soldiers and warriors for Him in the battle against His enemies." I then proceeded to quote the whole scripture to her from Isaiah 40:31: "'But they that wait upon the Lord shall renew their strength, they shall mount up with wings as eagles. They shall run and not be weary, they shall walk and not faint.' That's for *us* Heather. God meant that for *us*."

Her face lit up. "Oh, Grandma," she said with joy in her voice, "I love that! Teach it to me, please, so I can hide it in my heart and then I can take it out whenever I need it." Glory to God. She saw the bigger picture.

As the Holy Spirit continued to give me the wisdom to deal with the different situations that came up with Heather, each time I explained some spiritual concept to her, I was also saying to myself, "Yes. . .that's right. . .Wow, it's clear, even to me now. . ." And that's how He taught us.

Through all my learning experiences with Heather, I now understand so much more why Jesus said we have to come to Him as little children. They are incredible. They have a far greater capacity for understanding the things of God than most adults give them credit for. There's such a purity in their faith. I am so blessed to have Heather, because in teaching spiritual principles to her, my own faith has grown and solidified. Seeing her reactions to hearing the Word has helped me over many a difficult time. Only God could have thought to put the two of us together like that. It doesn't really matter how many years we have behind us, we are really all little children. God's children.

Sometimes we wonder why God doesn't answer a prayer the way we want it answered. We will probably never know the reason, and even when we do it won't matter. Although I may never understand, He remains sovereign. Often we question His ways, but some day we will know everything, and then we will no longer have to ask Him anything. It is difficult to know what to do while we're waiting and the answer is slow in coming, but I've learned that although He may not do it according to my time schedule, His timing is perfect. God is never too early, He's never late, but He's always right on time.

His Grace Is Sufficient

"For My thoughts are not your thoughts, neither are your ways My ways," declares the Lord. "As the heavens are higher than the earth, so are My ways higher than your ways and My thoughts than your thoughts. As the rain and the snow come down from heaven, and do not return to it without watering the earth and making it bud and flourish so that it yields seed for the sower and bread for the eater, so is My word that goes forth from My mouth; it will not return to Me empty, but will accomplish what I desire and achieve the purpose for which I sent it."

—Isaiah 55:8–11 (NIV)

*A*s we read in the Bible, Paul cried out to God three times, "Please, Lord, take this thorn from my flesh," but the Lord told Paul that His grace was sufficient for him, for His strength is made perfect in our weakness. On the road to Damascus, this man saw Jesus face to face; he was even taken up to heaven and saw things that were unspeakable for him to utter, and still he had to go through all kinds of trials and suffering. When I think about that, I say, "You're right, God. Your thoughts are not our thoughts, and Your ways are not our ways either. Yet, I love how Your Word really does go forth and accomplishes whatever You want it to accomplish. There's great joy in that."

This was the attitude of my heart when my daughter Jacqueline died. Even in the face of death and in the midst of pain, I was able to draw on that joy and say to Him, "I want You to know that I *love* You, Father. I will never understand why You do things the way You do them. You don't always answer my prayers the way I want them answered, either. But, in the great, overall plan that only You can see and I can't, I know You do it right. I don't understand You and I do get disappointed, Lord, but I love You."

In September of 1992, I received a heart-wrenching call from a hospital in New Brunswick, New Jersey. The nurse was courteous but business-like as she said, "Your daughter, Jacqueline, has been here in the hospital for several days in Intensive Care. Twenty minutes ago she went into respiratory arrest and we've been sustaining her by CPR, but she has just gone into cardiac arrest. We now have to do an invasive procedure, and we need your authorization."

My voice was calm and steady as I mechanically gave my permission, but my body was trembling and my heart pounding wildly as I hung up the telephone. I felt as though my innards were being torn out. This was my child they were talking about. This was my baby.

Jacqueline was twenty-eight years old. She was beautiful and bright, but for too many years she had been a severely addicted drug user. From time to time I had to fight the fear and dread of getting the kind of news I had just heard. Given her lifestyle, deep in my heart I knew that some day it might very well come to this point. I had not seen her for over five years and up until a few months before this call, there had been no contact for over two-and-a-half years. All that time I never knew where she was, but I thank God Jesus did!

During the five years of her absence, we had spoken occasionally on the telephone and whenever she called, I could tell that her situation was getting worse. She always called collect from a public telephone, and even when her father died, there had been no way of contacting her.

Jacqueline had given her heart to Jesus while watching a television evangelist one day when she was in her teens. She had also been baptized in the Holy Spirit. However, her life had taken a sudden turn, and now she had made too many wrong choices and strayed too far off the path to find her way back. From time to time I would remind her of her commitment to Jesus, and one day she said to me, "Mom, get off my back, will you? Look, I know God has a plan for my life and a path for me to follow. So, if I digress from the path, don't worry. I'll always be able to get back on. And another thing, stop always trying to help me. If I fall and break my face, it's my face. Stop always trying to put your fingers underneath my chin to cushion the fall."

I got so very sad and answered, "But I love that face, Jackie. And in some ways it's my face, too, 'cause you're mine."

"No, it's not!" she snapped, "It's mine! So back off!"

How I prayed that the Lord would help her come to the end of herself. It never happened. Not because God isn't able, but because her free will was involved, and God never interferes with our free will. Oh, He may have predestined us to be one of His special children, but the final decision as to whether we want to follow Him is up to us.

My one consistent prayer was that the Lord would give Jacqueline the chance to make her final peace with Him and to please not let her die without giving me an opportunity to pour out my love to her. He did. He is so faithful that He gave us the last four days of her life together. We serve a merciful God.

Within minutes after the call came, I made some necessary telephone calls and arranged a sitter for Heather. Then I drove to the City to pick up my daughter Christine and we headed for New Jersey. Correction: We didn't drive— we flew! It was one of those times in life that I found myself somewhere and, although I had been driving, I couldn't remember how I got there. Nevertheless by the time we arrived at the hospital, Jacqueline was still alive but she had lapsed into a coma.

Years before I had a friend who was in a coma for five months. I remembered her telling me that she could hear everything going on around her, except when she was sleeping. She said that although she always looked the same outwardly, on the inside sometimes she was awake and sometimes she was sleeping. When people came into the room and began talking to her, my friend said she would wake up and could hear everything. Inside she was reasoning perfectly and carrying on a full conversation, only nothing was coming out on the outside. I cannot imagine what a horrible prison that must be.

Armed with this knowledge, Christine and I approached Jacqueline as though she was fully awake. We announced our arrival to make sure she knew we were there, and we both took turns talking with her, telling her how much we loved her and how we had never stopped. We told her all about Heather, who was by then seven years old, and what a wonderful little girl she was. I reassured Jacqueline how much Heather loved her and how I had never bad-mouthed or said a contrary word about her to her daughter. I told her how very painful the tough-love approach had been on me because in my heart I yearned to continue the open-armed, openhearted, relationship we had before her addiction had gotten out of control.

It was important for me to explain to Jacqueline that although my intentions were good, by continually trying to make things better for her, I had been getting in God's way. I simply hadn't been able to watch her suffer when she was down, until the day finally came when I was strong enough to say, "No more." Up until that time, no matter what she did or how she came and went, no matter how much inner rage I had toward her, I had still tried to be loving and forgiving. I desperately wanted to keep the door of communication open between us, yet the problem was that all the while I was enabling her to continue living her lifestyle. The tough-love position had been very difficult but, painful or not, it was the only way. She knew it and I knew it. Although I had finally come to a place where I rejected her behavior, I wanted her to know I had not rejected *her*.

Sharing these things with Jacqueline was not easy, but it was necessary. I recalled Jesus' words, which tells us to make peace with our fellow man while we are on the way with him. Both Christine and I knew the time was short and there would never be another chance, so we poured out our hearts to her. Between the three of us, there was a lot of forgiving and asking for forgiveness that had to be done. There were too many open wounds that needed healing. On five separate occasions during our talks, tears poured out of Jacqueline's eyes and down the sides of her face as we shared poignant memories and moments of love.

During those four days, Christine and her husband came to the hospital every day and went back to New York each night. That gave me lots of time to spend alone with Jacqueline. Although I wasn't always sure whether she was awake and could hear me, I poured the Word of God and my love into her hour after hour. By the end of the first day, she had gone into complete kidney failure, and the doctors said that, at most, she only had about eighteen hours to live. Much to everyone's surprise, she lived on for three more days.

The next afternoon a lady minister affiliated with the hospital came by to talk to Christine and me. She said that earlier in the day before Jacqueline had gone into respiratory arrest, she had called for her. Jackie had told her, "I feel so afraid. I don't know what it is, but I have a strange feeling. Something I can't quite put my finger on. I think maybe today I'm going to die. . .and I'm scared. My life hasn't been what it should have been. Please pray with me. I want to make my peace with God." She did. They prayed, and Jackie took communion from the minister. Praise God for His faithfulness and for the indwelling Holy Spirit. He ministered repentance, contrition, and reconciliation to her before it was too late. That's the incomparable mercy of God.

After the minister left, I began talking to Jacqueline about the Lord and reminded her of the commitment she had made to Him. I told her, "Jackie, I think you'll agree it's time to rededicate your life to Jesus. I know you can hear me, and although you can't speak on the outside, I know you can repeat the words to God on the inside. It's what's in your heart that counts."

My voice was heavy with emotion as I said the prayer of salvation, pausing after each line, and giving her time to repeat it to herself. Both Christine and I could actually feel the presence of the Holy Spirit in that room and it was obvious that He was ministering to Jackie because it was one of the times she wept. When we were finished, we began thanking and praising God for His mercy. Chris was holding her sister's hand and said, "Oh Jackie, how I wish you could give us some kind of a sign that you can really hear everything we're saying to you." With that, the oscilloscopes monitoring Jackie's vital signs went crazy as she applied pressure with her two middle fingers into the palm of Christine's hand. We went a little crazy, too, laughing and crying at the same time. Not only had she heard us, but incredibly, God had given her the ability to summon every ounce of inner strength and respond.

For the next few days and nights the nurses and hospital staff were wonderfully kind and let me sleep in the small waiting room outside of the Coronary Care Unit. They let me shower, brought me coffee and sandwiches from time to time, and allowed me free access to her room at any hour. That gave me many opportunities to talk with them about God, especially during the late-night shift when they were caring for Jacqueline's physical needs. It was often during those times we were aware she was listening and could really hear us. Consequently, I was able to minister the Word both to them and to her. By watching the lights on the respirator and other monitoring machines, we could tell when she was fully alert and taking everything in, because her heart and pulse rates were up and she was breathing on her own.

As the days dragged on, a strange ambivalence took place in me. Her being alive became precious beyond anything but, at the same time, a nightmare. On the one hand I was praying for a last-minute miracle, and on the other, that God would please take her Home and put an end to her suffering. I knew He had a divine purpose in all that was going on, even if I didn't understand it. Divine purpose or not, it was still a nightmare.

On the night before Jacqueline died, Christine had already gone home, and I remained in the room until the early morning hours. Around one o'clock in the morning, I had come out for a little breather and possibly to catch a few winks of sleep. As I looked around, the woman in the next room lifted her hand weakly and waved. I smiled and waved back as she asked, "Would you please talk to me? I'm so lonely."

"Sure," I said, and I went in and stood at her bedside.

Her name was Martha and she was seventy-four years old. She was a pleasant woman, and we talked for almost half an hour about her family, and especially about her sisters, one with whom she had not spoken for over twenty years. Eventually, I brought Jesus into the conversation and asked if she had ever entered into a personal relationship with Him. She said she hadn't, so I gently led her through the prayer of salvation, and she gave her heart to the Lord. By this time I was no longer sleepy, so instead of napping I went back into my daughter's room. Although I was physically exhausted, my spirit was elated. I wanted to share what had happened with Jackie, but when I looked at her pathetic body in that bed, I couldn't say a word.

Watching her was, for me, an agony. I know that spiritually, death for the Christian is a joyful passage from this life into the next, but in the physical, dying means machines, tubes, and terrible suffering both for the person and for those looking on as well. This was the second time in my life I was watching one of my children go through this dreadful process. Doors to pain from the death of my daughter, Laura, that had been closed for so many years were once more opened wide. The flood of pain was almost more than I could bear. It seemed unbelievable that a body could be going through all she was going through and still be alive. And this wasn't just a body. This was my child, my own flesh and blood—my Jacqueline.

As I looked at her lying in the bed, I couldn't imagine what was keeping her alive. I thought, *My God, how I love her. I don't know, God, do I love her too much? Is there such a thing as loving your child too much? Is there?* I turned my attention back to Jacqueline and said, "I don't know if you are holding on to life for yourself or for me, Jackie, but on the chance you are doing it for me, I'm going to release you."

Tears streamed down my face as I continued, "I'm going to have to let you go, and I'm going to say to you the same words I had to say to your sister, Laura, before she died. Go! Leave this sick body behind. It's no longer serving you. The doctors don't know what is keeping you alive and neither do I. But if you're holding on for me, Jackie, don't hold on any longer. I let you go. You've made so many hard journeys in your life and this will be the most difficult one you will ever have to make."

Suddenly I recalled that she had told the minister a few days earlier she was afraid, so I went on, "And you don't have to be afraid, Jackie. Just know Jesus loves you and He said He will never leave you nor forsake you. I've asked Him to send angels of light to guide you over that River Jordan. I know He'll do that for you. Cross over, Jackie. You'll be whole. You'll be healed. You'll have joy and you'll be in perfect peace, something you haven't known for years. And you'll see Jesus, and Daddy, he's up there, and Laura, and Little Grandma. They'll all be there, waiting to greet you. . ." Great sobs wracked my body now as I added, "I love you with all my heart, but I love you enough to release you. Go and be with God. Some day, my dearest Jacqueline, when it is my turn, I'll see you again. And what a day that will be—no more tears, no more suffering, no more separations. We'll be together again, forever." As I finished, tears were rolling down both sides of her cheeks as well.

I spent the rest of the night next to her, holding her hand, and by early morning, I was distraught. I was kneeling on the floor next to her bed, wailing, "Why, God? Why is she still alive? She's already rededicated her life. So there's nothing left for her to do. Then it must be me! What haven't I done? What haven't I read or quoted or said that You want me to say? Who haven't I spoken to? I've talked about Your love and mercy to everybody here. What more do You want from me? What *do* You want? Please tell me! And please don't make it some nebulous message that I have to try to figure out. Please make it clear to me because I'm too dull, too tired, too stupid, or too whatever to know what You want. You have to tell me. Please. . .tell me what You want."

I was crying so hard that one of the nurses came in and suggested I go out and try to get some rest. While she was speaking to me, I suddenly became aware of a lot of commotion coming from next door. As I stepped out into the ward, I saw a whole group of people inside the room hovering around the bed, and everybody was crying. One woman was outside, leaning against the door, sobbing. Her grief touched me so deeply that I put my hand on her arm and asked, "Is she dying?"

"Yes, she is. She's my sister," came the tearful reply.

I said, "It's terrible losing someone you love, I know. You must love her very much."

She nodded. "Have you told her that?" I asked.

The woman answered, "I do love her, but I can't tell her because we haven't spoken for years." This was the sister Martha had talked about! She continued, "I've *never* told her I love her, so what good would it do now? She's in a coma and she can't hear me."

I said, "Oh yes, she can. My daughter is in a coma, and I know she can hear everything I say to her. In fact, your sister and I were talking last night and she mentioned all her sisters. I'm sure she'd be so happy for you to go in and tell her."

With that, her whole expression changed. "What are you talking about?" she snapped, "She couldn't have talked with you last night. She's been in a coma for five days."

"Well, that may be," I answered, "but all I know is that she was awake last night and we talked for almost half an hour. In fact, she prayed with me and gave her heart to Jesus. Do you know that when she leaves this world, she's going to be in the very presence of God? I know you are terribly sad, but there really is joy in knowing she's going right to heaven, don't you think?"

"You're crazy!" she shot back, angrily. *"You didn't talk to her last night* and *she can't hear me."*

Now, she really got to me. I know that when I accepted Jesus I was delivered from under the *dominion* of sin, but God still had a lot of work to do on my human nature. We were still standing by the door when she insisted her sister couldn't hear us, so I said, "Get out of my way!" and walked right past her into the room. I stood next to the bed and said in a loud voice above the din, "Martha!"

Without opening her eyes, the woman in the bed turned her head toward my voice and said, "What?"

At that, everybody gasped and the room got quiet. I continued, "It's me, Carole, the woman who prayed with you last night. Your sister is here and she wants to tell you how much she loves you." With that, I stepped away and said to the sister, "Go and tell her that you love her." As I walked out the two of them made their peace and, within minutes, Martha went Home to be with the Lord. One more example of the fact that it is never too late with God. Glory!

Oh, what a mighty God we serve. I get excited just thinking about how He works His extraordinary ways in the midst of our most ordinary circumstances. In all the excitement, I had almost forgotten that when I was crying earlier I had asked the Lord to show me what it was He wanted me to do. I forgot, but thank God, He didn't.

It was now about 6:30 A.M. As I walked down the hall, I came to the room of a thirty-nine-year-old man named Ed. He smiled and asked how my daughter was doing, and I just shook my head and told him it was only a matter of time. I had seen Christine and her husband in there a couple of times, and I apologized to him for not having stopped in sooner. I inquired as to his well being and then he asked how I was doing. I answered, "Oh, I'm all right. I'm strong in the Lord and in the power of His might."

"Gee," he said, "you're lucky. I don't know anything about God. You see I'm Jewish."

I thought to myself, *I really don't know what that has to do with it. If anything, you should know more about God because you are one of His chosen people.*

He went on. "My parents never taught us anything about God. They said when we got older we could make our own choices. I guess I never really did."

At the very instant he said he was Jewish, the Holy Spirit flashed a line of scripture across my mind. I said to Ed, "You know, I was just in my daughter's room crying out to God, asking Him why He hadn't taken her Home yet and what hadn't I done that He wanted me to do. Just now when you said you were Jewish, a line from the Bible, from the Book of Esther, came into my mind. It's from a story in the Old Testament when all the Jews were in danger of being massacred. Queen Esther was in the king's palace, and she was being called to intercede for her people. A man named Mordecai told her that perhaps she had come to that place for that specific time and purpose.

I continued, "Maybe that applies to me as well. Perhaps it is for a time such as *this* that *I* have come to this place. Tell me, Ed, has anyone ever told you that Jesus is Messiah?"

He said no, and, starting with the Old Testament, I proceeded to talk about the covenants and explained to him God's wonderful plan of salvation. One-and-one-half-hours later, this young man was weeping softly and repeating the salvation prayer with me. Hallelujah!

Later that afternoon, I kissed Jacqueline for the last time, and she went Home to be with God. As we were leaving the ward and were passing Ed's room, he called out to me. With tears streaming down his face he said, "Goodbye, Carole. Goodbye. You know, I will probably never see you again down here, but I'll see you up there." He was beaming with joy and pointing to the sky. "And I'll remind you of this day. And even though I never met your daughter, when I get to heaven I'll give her such a hug and tell her, 'You know, when you were in the hospital, dying, I was in the hospital too, and your mom prayed with me. And the day you died, I got eternal life.'" Glory! What joy! He really got it. He had a true and immediate conversion experience. He was saved down to the marrow of his bones.

What can I say to all of this? Do I understand God's ways? No. I only know that in spite of all the sadness, His Word went forth and accomplished all that He meant for it to accomplish. In every possible way, His plan was fulfilled. We serve an awesome God. His Word *is* truth, and worth repeating here that just as the rain and the snow come down they water the earth, causing it to bud and flourish and yield seed for the sower and bread for the reaper. Sometimes the path He chooses for us is one we would never have chosen for ourselves. Although the journey is rough and hard, He walks side by side with us, and all along the way we find His grace *is* sufficient.

Just for Laughs

A merry heart doeth good like a medicine.
—Proverb. 17:22

*S*ometimes there is a story to tell that you know isn't really going to change anyone's life, but it's worth the telling simply because it's funny and everyone can use a good laugh from time to time. The Word says that a happy heart works like a medicine. There have been times when I've known I just laughed myself into six more months of good health. Who knows? It could happen to you.

This is a true story which took place in 1978, when Jacqueline was still living with us and our home life was pleasant. In those days on Saturday nights we always watched the *Late* and the *Late Late Shows* on television until the wee hours of the morning. This night was no exception.

All evening long I had been sitting there totally distracted. I was playing with a piece of thread with my tongue and making a suction-y, click-y, sort of noise with my mouth. In frustration, Rudy finally asked, "Just what are you doing? I've been listening to you do that all night, and I'm tired of hearing it."

I laughed, but then said, apologetically, "Gee, I'm sorry, but I'm so uncomfortable with these gums of mine. You know I had surgery at the periodontist on Thursday, and now my gums are itching me like mad. What's worse, he left all these long pieces of thick, black suturing thread wrapped around my teeth after the surgery, and now some pieces of the thread have come loose and are hanging down on my tongue."

Rudy and Jackie both started to grin. "To make matters even worse," I continued, "the dentist said not to brush on that side of my mouth till tomorrow. You know how neurotic I am about brushing my teeth. Now, I don't know if my gums are itching because they are beginning to heal or if the itching is being caused by germs doing their thing. And whatever their thing is, I don't want them doing it on my gums."

Their grins widened and Rudy said, "Well, just stop it, okay?"

For the rest of the night I couldn't wait for the second movie to end so I could do something to get rid of the itching. I *am* neurotic when it comes to keeping my teeth clean, and it was very upsetting to me that I wasn't allowed to brush for three full days. I kept imagining all these squillions of germs doing whatever germs do, and I just had to put a stop to it. But how? Suddenly, I got what I thought was a brilliant idea. *I know what I'll do,* I thought, *I'll gargle my mouth with peroxide. That should do it. After all, if peroxide kills the bacteria on a cut, it can certainly kill what's in my mouth as well.*

I quietly slipped out of the room and went into the bathroom, filled the eight-ounce bathroom cup with peroxide and was just about to take a mouthful, when Jackie came walking in. "What are you doing?" she asked.

"Well, I told you my gums have been itching me like crazy," I said, "so I figured if I gargle with peroxide it will kill the germs and stop the itch."

Meanwhile, Jackie had picked up the bottle and was reading the label. She said, "It says here that this is poisonous if it's ingested and that you should call Poison Control if you drink it."

"I don't intend to drink it, Jackie, I'm only going to gargle with it," I answered.

"Well," she continued, "I still think that if it's poisonous to drink, maybe you shouldn't put it in your mouth, either."

At that point I put the glass down on the counter and said, "For goodness sake, Jackie, stop making such a big deal out of this. All I want to do is get some relief from the itching."

"I still think you shouldn't do it. It might be dangerous." she answered. Then looking back at the label, she added, "You know, this is dumb. They say here that if you do drink it you should call Poison Control. So why don't they put the number of Poison Control on the label? I mean, what are you supposed to do if you do swallow it? Call the operator and say, 'Oh, excuse me, Operator, but I just poisoned myself. If you're not too busy, do you think you could give me the number of Poison Control?'"

"No, you silly," I said. "Do you know how many poison control centers there are in America? They would need a label as big as a wall to list them all. What you do is call Information and ask for the number of your local Poison Control and hope you get to *them* before the poison gets to *you*."

While we were talking, my husband came walking by and asked, "Do you know it's almost two-thirty in the morning? What are you two talking about?"

"Oh, no!" I groaned. "Don't tell me I have to go through this whole stupid conversation all over again. For heaven's sake! The long and short of it is this: My gums are itching from the surgery. I think it's being caused by germs. All I want to do is gargle with peroxide to kill the germs, but she doesn't think I should because it's poisonous."

"Well, maybe she's right," he said, "Maybe you should just take an aspirin. If aspirin is good for pain, maybe it's good for itching, too."

"Oh, all right," I said, giving up. So, I opened the medicine cabinet, took out two tablets, popped them into my mouth, picked up the glass from the counter, and *drank the peroxide!*

The amazing thing is that I drank the whole glass and never even tasted it until the very last gulp had gone down. Now, as soon as the peroxide hit all the smooth linings of the throat and all the rest of the passageways down to my stomach, it started to bubble. I suddenly became keenly aware of several of my internal organs. Wherever it landed, I had a sensation that was a combination of burning and itching at the same time. Whatever it was, I couldn't stand it. I didn't know what to do with the feeling and I couldn't speak because my throat was burning, so I began stomping my foot on the floor.

At that point, Jackie realized what I had done and screamed, "Oh my God, she drank the peroxide."

"Awww, she did not." Rudy said, incredulously. I couldn't speak, but in order to assure him that I had, indeed, done this brilliant thing, I forced some air out of my throat and began making this unbelievably loud noise, sounding something like the mating call of a moose. To emphasize my dilemma I stomped my foot even harder, began shaking my head, and started making wild waving gestures with my finger pointing at my throat. "Oh my God," he said, "she *did* drink it."

Now, Jackie sprang into action. She dashed into the kitchen and I could hear her screaming into the telephone, "What do you mean, 'hold on'? My mother just poisoned herself and you're telling me to 'hold on?'" Once she got connected to Poison Control, I could hear her explaining the situation to them and she began relaying the information back to me. "Mom, they said to start drinking water. As much as you can get into you. They'll hold on the phone with me while you're doing it." I was not about to offer an argument, so I began drinking one glass of water after another. Just about the time I thought I would burst, Jackie called from the kitchen and said, "They said when you feel you can't drink any more, put your finger down your throat and make yourself throw up."

Well, I could have put Yellowstone Park's Old Faithful to shame. As soon as my finger touched my tongue, not even anywhere near my throat, up came everything. That stuff came shooting out of me like a rocket. The problem was it came up with such a force that some of it shot out through my nose. As if the burning itch every place else wasn't enough, now it was in my nose as well. To add to the idiocy of the scene, I grabbed onto my nose and resumed stomping my foot, all the while making these loud honking noises. For the first time I realized what uncanny talent I had for making animal sounds. It really sounded like a flock of geese!

In the meantime, Jackie had been explaining to Poison Control what was going on with me. They said the fact that my nose was burning wasn't important. I thought, *Easy for them to say. They don't have the burning.* They said as long as I had gotten everything up there was nothing to worry about and that if the burning didn't let up or if I still couldn't stand it, I should go to the emergency room. After all I had been through I was not going to any hospital. I was afraid that when they heard my story, God knows *what* ward they might have put me in.

For quite a while Rudy and Jackie kept asking how I was, and I kept telling them I was fine, but it wasn't true. Although the sensation was subdued, I could still feel the burning. Finally, I took the phone into my bedroom closet so they wouldn't hear me and secretly called Poison Control myself. I explained who I was and what I had done and asked if there was anything else I could possibly do to alleviate the discomfort other than going to the hospital. They said, "Sure. Just drink a glass of milk." *A glass of milk? Why didn't they say that in the first place?* Sure enough, as soon as I drank it, except for my nasal passages, all the bubbling sensation went away.

Needless to say, when the humor of the whole situation hit us, there was no sleeping for the rest of the night. At one point I heard this gasping sound coming from the hall and when I looked, there was Rudy leaning against the wall, bent in half and spastic with laughter. Whenever the house got quiet, every once in a while from either bedroom, we would hear uproarious laughter, and we would start in all over again. This went on till dawn.

I thank You, God, for laughter. It does "maketh good like a medicine." And I thank You, God, for happy times and happy memories.

Fighting for Life

I shall not die, but live, and declare the works of the Lord. The Lord hath chastened me sore: but He hath not given me over to death.
—Psalm 118:17

*I*t was one afternoon in June of 1993 that I was in the hospital once more, recovering from major surgery. I was propped up in bed and sat there smiling as the three oncologists walked into my room. The looks on their faces prompted me to ask, "What makes me think you are going to wipe this smile off my face?" My thinking was correct. They did.

One of the doctors who appeared to be the leader began, "We're so sorry to have to tell you this, Mrs. Rucci, but you had a malignant tumor called a liomyosarcoma, which is a very deadly type of cancer. The surgeon had to remove another section of your small intestine and, unfortunately, the tumor had already metastasized. This means it has spread to other organs of your body. Consequently, the surgeon also had to remove a small section of your liver."

As his voice droned on I heard the gravity of his words, but my mind refused to take them in. Instead, as I listened, the mocking voice inside my head was saying, "Got any more good news for me, Charlie Brown?" This is called denial.

The doctor continued to explain that the medical profession still had not found any chemotherapy or radiation that has ever had any degree of success with this particular type of cancer. He added, "Even as we speak, other cancerous 'seeds' are taking root and spreading throughout your body." He went on to describe the various places I should expect the sarcoma to hit my body next. Inasmuch as this was my second bout with cancer in less than five years, and it had advanced to the degree it had, he said it was only a matter of time before there would be another recurrence. He added that it was not a matter of years, but at the most, I only had a few months to live. They were sending me home to wait for the next set of symptoms, and they promised to keep me as comfortable as possible. He suggested that I put my affairs in order as quickly as I could, and added that, according to their records, I was classified as terminal.

By this time I was no longer making smart aleck remarks in my head. This was real. I sat there in silence; my heart sinking with every word he spoke. I thought, *Months? That's all they're giving me to live? This can't be. It just can't be!* I thought back on all the preceding months of debilitating fatigue and sickness, the dozens of painful and dehumanizing tests, the surgery, and the mental stress and torment for me, my family, and my friends. *And now, this?* I thought, *This is how it all ends?*

Although some people are definitely laid back and mellow, those who know me know that I am not. I am a fighter. As I stated earlier, in the family I grew up in, you either learned to fight or you didn't grow up. Right up to the present day when I feel backed into a corner, my tendency is to come out fighting. The difference is that now I use the Word of God to do my fighting. In that way I know I am no longer doing battle in my own strength but in the power of the Holy Spirit.

I waited for a lull in the doctors' conversation and finally I said, "Can I say something now?"

The "leader" said, "Yes, of course, Mrs. Rucci. What is it?"

"I hear what you are telling me," I said, "but I'm telling *you* that with God's help I'm going to beat this thing."

He smiled patronizingly and said, "Yes, Mrs. Rucci, we know."

"No! You *don't* know!" I snapped back at him.

Deliberately ignoring the intensity of my response, he answered, "Well, Mrs. Rucci, as we said, we'll keep you as comfortable as possible. . ."

"No," I interrupted, "I'm *telling* you! If it's God's will that I live, I'm going to beat this disease. You think this thing is going to get me? Well, it's not!"

In an attempt to placate me, he said "Yes, Mrs. Rucci, we hear you."

"No," I said, "you are not hearing me. You said I only have a few months to live, but the Word of God says that *He* has numbered my days, not you! And my days are written in *His* book, not yours."

Earlier that day a friend had called and told me to look up Psalm 118, verse 17. She said I should take that verse for myself because it was for *me*. I did. Remembering that scripture, I continued, "And there's one more Bible verse you should hear. It says, 'I shall not die but I shall live to declare the wondrous works of the Lord, for the Lord has chastened me sorely but He has not given me over to death.'"

By this time the doctors were fidgeting, tired of hearing me mention God. One of them said back to me, "Mrs. Rucci, God has nothing to do with this."

I shot back, "Nothing to do with this? No! God has *everything* to do with this! Because if He sucks the breath out of your body this very minute you are nothing but dead meat!"

I really don't think they expected that kind of an answer. They all grinned and the leader said, "You know, I think perhaps you *are* going to make it, but having nothing to do with God. I think you are just ornery enough to make it on your own."

We all laughed at this point as I added, "I tell you what. Every year on the anniversary of this surgery I am going to send you a card, just to let you know I'm alive and kicking. Deal?"

"Deal," they all answered. I have. Almost eight years have passed and each year I have sent them cards with long letters inside. In the next chapter you will see the card and read several of those letters. However, dear reader, I must make one confession here. Despite all my bravado in confessing and speaking out the Word of God, the minute those doctors left the room and I was alone, I turned my head into my pillow and wept.

That hospital stay lasted eighteen days and, once more, the time spent there was spiritually very fruitful. I had eleven roommates during that time, and eight of them asked Jesus into their hearts. I witnessed to everyone around me—patients, nurses, and even a few doctors.

Immediately after the surgery they had encouraged us to exercise by walking, and soon I began to make friends on my little walks through the corridors. On one of my walks, I had given a man a tract that had the salvation prayer on the back page, but for several days after that I did not see him. When I finally did, I was so pleased because it was like seeing an old friend. I was also anxious to find out if he had said the prayer. When I asked him, his whole countenance changed. He beamed and said, "I certainly did, and you have no idea what it has done for me. I read those scriptures over and over during all these days I couldn't get out of bed, and they have changed my life. You just don't know." His face was glowing. "You can't imagine. . ." I laughed and told him I *did* know and that what he was feeling was the joy of the Lord.

Whenever I am reading the Word, I have learned to ask the question, "What else is happening here besides what's happening here?" I try to find out what that particular scripture is saying to *me*. The same is true with my circumstances. I always try to look beyond the situation to discern what the Lord is doing through it. I knew He was somehow working out something of eternal value for me through this present situation, but I needed help to know what it was. I am not always sure when *I* should do something, or when I should sit back and wait on God to see what *He* is going to do. I know there are times He sovereignly heals people and at other times He doesn't. This condition was not some minor thing; I was fighting for my life. Waiting on God is always difficult, but it is even more so when dealing with a life and death situation. There was an urgency to this, and I needed help. It was not a time for either philosophical or theological discussions; it was a time for prayer.

I can remember talking with my pastor's wife at the time and saying to her, "I can't believe that I'm sitting here talking with you, and there's a possibility that within a few months I might be dead. And it's a funny thing, but I think it's the first time in my life I have ever really wanted to live. For so many years I felt so utterly trapped in my marriage and thought the only way out was to die. But now, I think I want to live."

You *think?*" she asked, "Why *do* you want to live, Carole?"

"Well," I answered, "I want to live for Heather, and for my daughter, Christine, and for all my friends who love me."

"What about *you?*" she asked, "Don't you want to live for *yourself?*" I sat back in amazement because I had never even thought of myself. She saw the look and continued,

"When you make up your mind that you want to live for *you*, that will determine whether or not you will live *at all*."

Later on, in the quiet hours of the night, I thought about all the times over the years I had secretly wished for death. Maybe to some people those thoughts are so foreign that they can't even conceive of anyone feeling that way. Those people are truly blessed. However, through my ministering to hundreds of women, I have found this is far more common than one would imagine. While pondering these things, I began to feel intense conviction from the Holy Spirit. For the first time I realized that wishing for death was sin. It was like wanting to throw God's precious gift of life back in His face. I cried, confessed, repented, and renounced that death wish before the Lord, and prayed for the grace to receive His love in greater measure. Then I prayed, "Please God, I want to live. Please let me live."

A few weeks after I came home from the hospital, Christine came to the house armed with a huge pile of books on nutrition, juicing, and alternative medicine. We also got books from the library about people who had been healed of cancer through methods other than traditional medicine. Inasmuch as there was no protocol for the type of cancer that had struck me, it seemed as though God was definitely pointing to some other avenue of treatment. I read all the information voraciously and then narrowed my choices down to two particular alternative cancer treatment doctors. At this point I put the choices on a shelf and waited for God to direct me.

However, there was one other very important aspect of this situation that could not be ignored. Inasmuch as this was my second bout with the disease, I had to start being good to my body in order to get healthy. It's a well-known fact that the American diet contributes greatly to the number of cancer cases, and I did some research and made several drastic dietary changes. It is true that a merry heart does make good medicine so, other than the Bible, I only read humorous books and only watched funny videos that made me laugh. I did everything I knew while waiting to see to which doctor the Lord was directing me.

Now that I had taken steps to deal with some of the physical aspects of my problem, something needed to be done on the spiritual level. Although I had authored a book on intercessory prayer and spiritual warfare, I was not quite sure how this battle was to be fought. I simply went before the Lord and asked Him for a battle plan.

One night, a short while later, I was lying in bed thinking, praying, and talking to God about all that was happening. I thought about this devilish thing called cancer, and said aloud, "What a formidable foe. Like evil, itself, it goes along devouring and destroying." Then I thought of the scripture from 1 Peter 5:8, which says, "The devil, as a roaring lion, roameth about seeking whom he may devour."

That's a confirmation, I thought. *Just like evil, cancer goes about increasing and expanding itself at the expense of, and to the total consumption of, its victim. It fulfills no purpose other than to reproduce, consume, and to kill. But, for the body it is totally unproductive. . .*When I said the word *unproductive,* suddenly my thoughts jumped to the account in the Bible when Jesus and the disciples were on their way to Bethany. Jesus had cursed the fig tree and the next day they saw it had died at its roots. And the reason He had cursed it was because *it was unproductive!*

For years I had never understood that scripture or why the story was in the Bible to begin with. In my ignorance I used to think, *What did that fig tree ever do to You, Jesus? Why did You curse it and make it die? I mean, Your Word tells us in black and white, it wasn't even the season for figs. So why?* It simply didn't make any sense to me. Later I learned that it is not enough to only look fruitful, but we have to be productive and bear spiritual fruit. The tree had all the outer signs of bearing fruit, but in reality had none to offer. It is like some Christians who talk the talk but who do not walk the walk; they have lip, but no life; who look like believers, but are make-believers. The painful truth is, if we do not bear fruit, we will be cut off. I often say to the Lord with a little bit of a grin, "You don't fool around, do You, God? Please help me to never cross You or to be unfruitful. Okay?"

While I was mulling the scripture over in my mind, suddenly the Word became alive to me. My heart began pounding and my mind was racing. The doctors had talked about the disease making new *roots*. Jesus cursed the fig tree *at its roots* and by the very next day *it was dead*. Of course, that was it! That was my battle plan. Glory!

The counter attack began. First I praised and thanked the Lord for Who He is, for all He does, and for who I am in Him. Then I started to do warfare. I said, "Father God, in the name of Jesus Christ, my Lord and Savior, I now curse this cancer at its roots. In the name of Jesus and by the power in the Blood, I speak to this cancer and say that you must die, and you must die *at your roots*. Every cancer cell within my body, you must die. In the authority of Jesus' name, once more I curse you at your roots and in Jesus' name I bind you, rebuke you, and command you to loose me now. You are a mountain in my life and you have invaded my body, but by the full and finished work of Jesus, I say you must be removed. In the name of Jesus, I deny you the authority to stay in my body. You must go! Now, Holy Spirit, I pray that You would cause my body to line up with the Word of God that says He took my sickness and infirmities and *by His stripes I am healed.*"

I then spent time praying for Jesus to *"life"* me. That is, to bring life to every part of my body. I asked Him to send forth His healing light into every darkened part. Then I asked the Holy Spirit to quicken every cell within me with the knowledge that it was being loved to life by Jesus, so that His healing power would become effective. I asked Him, "Love me to life, Lord, and then *life* me, that I may love." I did this type warfare against the enemy every night. Whenever I heard the "doom tapes" start to play in my head, I told that devil to shut up in Jesus' name. Whenever the fear began to well up in me, I did warfare. I even came against the spirit of *fear of cancer.* I often fell asleep praising God and thanking Him ahead of time for my healing and for all He was doing in my life.

Early one morning about a week later, I was reading about King Hezekiah in the Bible. When the enemy had written the letter threatening him and the Israelites, he brought the letter into the temple and laid it down on the ground before the Lord. Then the Lord answered him and told him what he should do.

Later that morning I went to the intercessory prayer meeting at church and took some papers with me regarding one of the doctors. I had read about so many different alternative cancer treatment plans and I felt the Holy Spirit was directing me to this one particular physician. However, I was still waiting for a confirmation. As the meeting was about to end, I asked permission to place the papers on the floor as Hezekiah had done. We then prayed for wisdom and direction.

That day I had an appointment with a friend who lives four towns from the church, and we drove two towns farther away to have lunch. While we were waiting for our order, I was talking to my friend about the decision I had to make soon. I was in the midst of telling her that I had narrowed my choice down to one particular doctor in Manhattan, but never mentioned his name. As we sat there, a woman from behind us interrupted our conversation and said, "Who are you talking about? Doctor Revici?"

Tears sprung to my eyes as I turned to her and answered, "Yes, as a matter of fact, that is exactly who I am planning to see. What do you know about him?"

"He's the best," she said, "I don't think you could have made a better choice."

What a mighty God we serve! Can you believe it? What are the chances that out of the thousands of doctors in New York City, a total stranger in a town I've never been to before, should come up with the very name of the man I was considering? Only God could have done that. What a confirmation! God is awesome! Oh, I am so ashamed of myself when I am even tempted to doubt Him. He is such a loving Father Who takes such good care of His children.

Throughout this ordeal God was truly our Provider in every sense of the word. Every one of our needs was met. Prior to the surgery, when I had been too sick and too weak to function, friends had come to the house early in the morning to give Heather breakfast and get her ready for school. Another friend took a one-month leave of absence from her job, and she and her husband took care of Heather all the while I was in the hospital and while I was convalescing. When I came home, another friend slept at the house for a full week to take care of me. Women from our church made a schedule and every night for two months, someone showed up with a fully cooked meal. It took a lot of loving care on their part because all the meals were in keeping with my new diet plan, which meant no red meats and lots of vegetables. People sent fruit baskets, flowers, financial blessings, and over fifty cards and letters came to the house. Most of all, they prayed. How I thank God for the Body of Christ. I believe it was the prayers of the faithful that reached the throne room of God. He heard, and He answered. Bless His name.

I feel the need to say that although my particular battle plan worked for me, it is not being mentioned here as a formula for everyone else to follow. Through prayer, each person must find their own. Nevertheless, eight years have passed and, despite one last bout with cancer four years ago, I am still alive and well. I continue to stand on the scriptures that speak life to me. I teach them to others at meetings, conferences, retreats, and everywhere I go. I tell of the wondrous works of the Lord and how He has not given me over to death. Often I quote Psalm 118 as well as Jeremiah 29:11, which says, "For I know the plans that I have for you, declares the Lord, plans for good and not for evil, plans to prosper you and not to harm you, plans to give you hope and a future." (NIV). God has certainly done that and more. I fought for my life, and through His mercy and grace, I got the victory.

"I Made It!" - Cards Number 1–4

*The righteous will flourish like a palm tree. . . .they will
still bear fruit in old age, they will stay fresh and green,*
—Psalm 92:12–14 (NIV)

*I*n the last chapter, you might recall the conversation I
had with three oncologists who were giving me the not-
so-good news that the cancer was a deadly sarcoma, it
had spread to my liver, and that my life expectancy would
not exceed four months. I am firmly convinced that although there are all kinds of spiritual gifts, some of them
come from the wrong spirits. Let's just say those doctors
had the "gift of discouragement."

At that time I told them I was going to send a card every
year on the anniversary of the surgery just to let them know
I was still alive and kicking. Christine, and a friend named
Lloyd, did the cover. He scanned in a snapshot of my face
and Chris drew the figure. Gorgeous, huh? Each year I simply change the number on the sweatshirt to chart my survival record. As of this writing, I am anticipating card
number eight! Hallelujah! Is God good, or what?

Following are the cards. The letters speak for themselves,
as I tried to share my heart with the doctors.

"I Made It!" — Card #1

June 12, 1994

Hi there,

I'm Carole Rucci. Remember me? Of course, some of you doctors have been seeing me regularly so you couldn't forget me even if you wanted to. Right? But to the others who haven't seen me for a while and, just in case the rest of you forgot, here's the scoop. If you recall, it was just a year ago that I was in your care for what seemed like just another chapter in the losing battle against cancer. I told you then that that "thing" was not going to get me, and that I was going to send you a card every year on the anniversary of the surgery just to let you know I'm alive and kicking. Well, here it is!

Just to fill you in, I am not only alive, but I am well. With the help of our wonderful God, Whom I love and serve with all my heart, I've been allowed to continue to raise my very active eight-and-one-half-year-old granddaughter, Heather, clean my house, do my gardening, travel, and do speaking engagements. And. . .(a drum roll, please) the piece de resistance is that last weekend I went white water rafting down the Lehigh Valley River. How's that for living?

How am I doing it? Well, spiritually, Jesus is Lord of my life. I have prayed to God for total healing and trust Him that He has answered my prayer. When a farmer wants to reap a harvest, he has to do his part in preparing the ground and planting the seed, but he has no control over its growth. God does that! Well, every day I do my part and God does the rest. On the physical side, I keep away from eating red meat, white flour, caffeine, most sugar and fats. Under the supervision of an alternative cancer treatment doctor, I'm taking selenium, magnesium, copper, sulfur, lipids, ketones, beta carotene, and other vitamins. Psychologically, I'm a fighter. Although I don't deny there's a mountain in my life, I refuse to give that mountain the authority to stay there. In Jesus' name I tell it that it must go! Again, in His name, I command the cancer to die at its roots and be gone from my body. Then I ask Jesus to "life" me—that is, to love me to life so I may serve Him all the rest of my days. It seems to be working, wouldn't you say? To God be the glory!

Anyway, that's who and where I am. . .and that's all for now. You'll be hearing from me again next year with the help of God. You know, it's funny. When I was young I asked God for all things that I might enjoy life. Now He has given me life, that I might enjoy all things. Thank you for being a fellow pilgrim for a part of my journey. I pray you and yours are well.

With warmest regards,

Carole

"I Made It!" — Card #2

June 16, 1995

Hi there,

Remember me? Well, another year has gone by since my surgery in 1993 and guess who, by the grace of God, is still alive and well? I am! As you can see, this year I'm sporting a shock of silvery hair.

I decided to "give up the bottle" and go "au natural."

To fill you in, with the help of God, I am still doing all the things required of me as a single (grand)parent raising my lovely nine-and-one-half-year-old granddaughter, Heather. I also clean my house, do the gardening, teach a Bible study in my home, do speaking engagements, and, in between times, have started writing another book. Not bad for someone whose prognosis was as poor as mine back in 1993.

I have many wonderful friends who are still faithfully praying for my continued good health. I, too, have been faithful in eating properly, taking all the vitamins, etc. prescribed by the alternative cancer-treatment doctor, keeping a good mental attitude of gratitude, and fighting anything that would rob me of the plan which the Lord has for my life.

Of course, all the good diet and vitamins in the world can't do what God is doing, for what is impossible to man is possible with God. It is because He strengthens me each day in my inner spirit that I am well and because I try to live each day according to the truths the Bible teaches.

Psalm 118, verse 17 is a scripture that has been foundational for me. It says, "I shall not die but I shall live to declare the wondrous works of the Lord, for the Lord has chastened me sorely but He has not given me over to death." It seems I'm living that out in my life, wouldn't you say?

By the way, if you remember, last year I told you that I had gone white water rafting down the Lehigh Valley River. It was so wonderful that next week, God willing, I am going again. Last year I had wished the rapids had been little rougher than they were, so this year, forty of us from our church are going on the day they open up the dams. Isn't God so wonderful to allow us to enjoy and share in the beauty of His creation? Want to come along? It'll be fun! We'll laugh ourselves into six months worth of good health.

Anyway, that's all for now. I hope you are happy for me at how good the Lord has been. The Bible tells us to "fight the good fight of faith" and that is what I have tried to do. I am so grateful that I seem to be winning the battle. But then, again, the odds are with me; for if God is on my side, the two of us together make a majority.

I pray you and yours are well, and that, perhaps, because of this sharing, you will glorify the Lord together with me.

Until next year, I send warm regards,

Carole

"I Made It!" — Card #3

June 15, 1996

Hi there,

Can you believe that another year has gone by? As you can see, I'm sporting a big #3 on my shirt, signifying, of course, that three years have passed and I'm still alive and well. My lovely granddaughter, Heather, is going to be eleven this year and she keeps me busy, young, and tired. About the time you read this I will, God willing, once more be white water rafting down the Lehigh Valley River with friends. Also, I've started mowing my own lawn this year and thanking God for the strength to be able to do it. In short, I'm so very grateful for every minute of my life.

I hope you are not getting bored with these cards. Then, again, do I really care if you are bored? *No!* In fact, I hope you get very, very bored getting these cards from me every year. Are you smiling? I am.

As you all remember, the circumstances under which we met were definitely not favorable to me. In fact, I was slated to become another statistic in the losing fight against cancer. However, by the grace of God He had other plans for me. I remember the oncologist who made the pronouncement about my not-very-promising life expectancy and how I said my days were written in God's Book and not in man's. I said that if it were the will of God that I live, then I would beat this formidable foe. So far it looks as though He still has lots of work for me to do, and I'm doing it. Beside all my other duties as mother/grandmother and homemaker, I teach the teenagers in my church on Sundays; have a Bible study in my home; speak, teach, and preach the Word of God at various churches, organizations, dinners, and meetings. It "aint" easy, but I love it.

So. . .why am I saying all this? Because I need to share my thoughts with you. While on the one hand I'm so happy to be alive, even if the Lord should call me home, I'm at peace because I know where I'm going. Do you? Have you given any thought to your having a relationship with your Maker? Have you thought about how powerfully He could use you in the special capacity you are in? How, as a doctor, you can instill faith in a prayer-answering God Who has promised to see them through the ordeals through which they are going?

When I began thinking about what to write this year, it occurred to me to share a life-long belief of mine. That is, whether it is a five-minute cab ride, a lifetime relationship, or a doctor-patient relationship like ours, we all become a part of each other's lives for a time.

A person can't give out what they don't have, can they? So...just in case you need it, I'm enclosing a small "tract" for you to read. There's a wonderful prayer on the back of it you might want to say so as to take the first step in a personal relationship with the Lord. It doesn't matter how far from Him you think you might be. He will meet you right where you are.

Another thought, don't you think it's time that the medical profession begins giving some serious attention to nutrition, vitamins, and alternative medicine as a viable approach to the treatment of cancer and other diseases? There are volumes of cases proving the validity of alternative treatment, and I, for one, am living proof that it does work. You are in a position to be able to give real hope, where, conventionally, there is no hope. Thank God I had my daughter and other friends who did that for me when I was going through my terrible ordeal back in 1993.

I referred to it as my "terrible ordeal" because in many ways, it was the pits. And yet, in many other ways I would not exchange the incredible gifts to my spirit, soul, mind, and body which came as a result of my having had those experiences.

I hope by now you are not really bored with this, because that is not my intention. You see, I've always been willing to run the risk of having someone get angry or annoyed with me if saying what I believe will, ultimately, be of great benefit in their lives. That is why I've shared all of this with you. Because I care!

When I think of what God has brought me through, I'm so very happy and grateful for everything. I hope and pray you are, too. I hope you take this letter and the enclosed prayer tract seriously. Maybe I get a little too deep and maybe it isn't the "thing to do," but, hey, we only live once and we've got to let His light shine through to light up other people's lives as well.

Well, that's it for this year. God willing, you'll be hearing from me again in '97. In the meantime, I pray you and yours will be well. I pray that you will acknowledge God in all you do, for that is great wisdom. I also pray the Lord will bless and keep you and make His face to shine upon you; that He will lift up His countenance upon you and grant you peace. It's all good "stuff," and it's ours for the asking. I pray you do.

God bless,

Carole

"I Made It!" — Card #4

June 14, 1997

Hello, my friends,

Isn't that nice. . .? that I can call you "friends"? Well, that's how I feel about you. Most of you have been such a large part of all I went through this past January—the surgery, the complications, and the healing—and I can't thank you enough for all you did for me. It's no secret that because the surgery was so massive, this time I almost didn't make it—and there almost wasn't a #4 card. I'm so glad there is. I know you are, too.

I don't think anyone was more surprised than I to find that there was another problem. I was so positive I was totally cured back in 1993 and never expected a recurrence. I believe that it was partially due to the fact that I got really "sloppy" with my diet in the last year, and had begun eating things I shouldn't have eaten. If ever there was proof needed that cancer is linked with a faulty diet, this was it. Presently, I am looking into a different alternative cancer treatment plan than what I have used these past few years.

I know that faith, by its very nature, must be tested, and this last attack from the enemy surely tried mine. Aside from all the physical things that were going on, spiritually, this was a time that I had to do some real "hanging in there." I'm sure you know that strong faith does not come in a bottle that says, "Strong Faith. Take One." But mine was built up by looking back on all God has done for me in the past and knowing that if He let me down this time it would be the very first time. I believe I am going to live and be well. After all, if the Lord wanted to take me home He has certainly had ample opportunity to do so, and He hasn't done it. Praise Him for that!

That is all in the past, and now I am going on with the business of getting healed and resuming life—the abundant life, that is. Once more I am planning to go white water rafting with a bunch of friends on the twenty-first, and this year I am taking my granddaughter along. She will be twelve and this 's probably the last year I can brag about being taller than she. I've been making use of all my recuperation time and am still working on writing a full-length book which I pray will be published some day. Just to let you know, I authored another book that now has forty-one thousand copies out. Not such a big deal, but it's enough.

I have also resumed teaching my home Bible study as well as teaching the teenagers at church. My schedule of speaking engagements is also pretty full and it looks as though the Lord still has lots of work for me to do.

I am not only alive but am loving my life. It's all in the attitude; and mine is an attitude of gratitude. I'm so very grateful to God to be alive and to be able to do all the things I am doing. I never take a single thing for granted and find joy in the most mundane of circumstances.

Even though the outside of me is getting older and has a few dents and bruises, inside I am younger and more vital than I have ever been. In the same way old trees grow new wood every year I, too, am endeavoring to grow "new wood" with each passing year. Much of what I have inside of me I try to pass on to others, and I am ever being replenished by God. Earlier in this letter I referred to what happened in January as another "attack." But for me, I consider it another victory.

I cannot close this letter without, once more, asking whether you have given any thought to having a personal relationship with the Lord. That is, if you do not already have one. I cannot tell you how important it is because those of us who study Bible prophecy are convinced that Jesus is coming soon. See? Once more I am making myself vulnerable and subject to ridicule. Do I care? No! When I get in front of the Lord some day I will stand before Him alone. So will you. Whatcha gonna do then?

In closing, I pray that you and yours are well and that the Lord will bless you at the level of your deepest needs. As for me, I pray for continued good health and that you will be hearing from me again next year. I am not afraid because, although I may not know what lies ahead, I know the One Who does. There may be more trials and problems, but I know He is going to carry me through. He will never leave me nor forsake me. Or you. He never has. He never will.

God bless,

Carole

I Don't Believe It! I Think. . .

For this we declare to you by the Lord's [own] word, that we who are alive and remain until the coming of the Lord shall in no way precede [into His presence] or have any advantage at all over those who have previously fallen asleep [in Him in death.] For the Lord Himself will descend from heaven with a loud cry of summons, with the shout of an archangel, and with the blast of the trumpet of God. And those who have departed this life in Christ will rise first. Then we, the living ones who remain [on the earth,] shall simultaneously be caught up along with [the resurrected dead] in the clouds to meet the Lord in the air; and so always (through the eternity of the eternities) we shall be with the Lord! Therefore comfort and encourage one another with these words.

—1 Thessalonians 4:15–18 (AMP)

*O*h, Mom, please," she moaned. "I don't want to hear it. I don't believe it and I don't want to hear about it, either." Christine all but put her hands over her ears to block out my words. Sarcastically, she added "Oh sure, it makes a lot of sense. Of course! Some day my mother and all her friends are going to hear a horn blow and they will all 'pouf' up into the sky and live happily ever after. Yep! What intelligent person can't believe something like that? The Rapture. . .please. . .let's not even talk about it because it's too ridiculous."

I felt so frustrated and stifled. I wanted to say, "You can get as angry at me as you want, but it's the truth. You won't be laughing if the Rapture comes tonight and you get left behind. Then you won't think it's funny." The very thought of that made me shudder.

At the time, Christine was not "into the Bible," as she put it. I couldn't stand the thought of her or anyone else I loved being left behind, and so whenever I saw an opening to bring up the subject, I did. I tried talking to her about the beauty of heaven and how she should at least think about the possibility of the Rapture really happening. She wanted no part of it. It was beginning to cause a serious rift between us, so after a while I learned to keep it to myself. There was nothing I could do but pray and wait for the right time to present itself.

For several years, Rudy and I had both taken a lot of ribbing from family and old friends because of our fundamentalist approach and belief in the Bible. Now that he was gone, it had intensified. One of the biggest subjects up for ridicule was that of the Rapture of the Church, which is described in the above scripture. I am one of the many Christians who are waiting in eager anticipation to hear the blast of the angel Gabriel's trumpet, and we're out of here!

Some people have accused me of being an escapist. Right! With all my heart, I am hoping the Rapture will happen in my lifetime. It's not as though I'm unhappy being here, but I love the thought that some day we will all leave this earth *together*. This seems a lot better to me than being picked off one at a time, causing so much sadness. No, it will happen joyously and, if I may use the term, "rapturously." To those of us who are saved, this is good news. To the others, it is not. At the same time, I keep praying that the Holy Spirit will do a quick work in all of our loved ones so that none of them will have to go through the Tribulation. Some people believe the Rapture will occur mid-way through the Tribulation and some believe it will happen at the end, but I refuse to get into *that* whole discussion. I'm just hoping Jesus is "Pre-Trib." That is, that the Rapture will occur before the Tribulation begins.

Earlier I had really tried listening to Christine to better understand her thoughts on the subject, and realized that at my age it is so much easier to be looking forward to the Rapture than it is for a younger person. There are some Christians who are not yet totally sold out to God and have not quite gotten the vision of the incredibly wonderful things awaiting us on the other side. For these people, there is a reluctance to part with this world and the things that are in it. They feel they will be missing out on all the things in life they still want. Although the Bible specifically warns against setting our affections on things below and tells us to set them on things above, Christine, like many others, neither wanted to hear about it nor did she want to discuss it. To her, the whole idea of the Rapture was just too bizarre to even be considered.

Waiting was difficult, as usual. I often found myself asking the Lord, "How long, Jesus? How long do I have to wait to be able to discuss the things of God with the people who mean the most to me? After all we've been through, what is it going to take?" At the time my relationship with Christine was not close. We both have very strong personalities and in some ways are very much alike. Over the years we often had situations which caused us to lock horns with one another. I longed for the time when she would fully embrace all the truths in the Bible and we would be able to share them. It finally came.

It was summer, and Heather and I had gone to Maryland for a week's vacation. Friends who live nearby then invited us to stay at their house for an additional week. I thought about calling Christine to tell her, but she was away on a business trip, so I decided to wait until we got home. Heather and I had just walked in the door when the telephone rang. It was my sister-in-law inviting us to spend a week with her family at their seaside vacation home in Orient Point. We decided to go. That same day I unpacked the suitcases, washed the clothes, repacked, and we were on our way once more. However, in all the rush, I forgot to call Christine.

We spent another lovely week vacationing, and by the time we got home I was terribly guilt ridden that in all that time I had never made contact with Chris. She couldn't call me because she had no idea where we were. Finally, I dialed her number, and when she answered and I said, "Hello," I heard a loud gasp.

Christine's voice was shrill as she screamed into the telephone. "Oh, it's *you.*"

"What's wrong?" I asked, excitedly. My mind began racing with the thought that perhaps, while I was gone, something terrible had happened. I wondered if she had been trying to communicate with me all this time.

"Oh, it's really you," she sobbed, ignoring my question.

Again, I asked, "What's wrong, Chrissie, is everything all right? Has something happened?"

"No," she said, "nothing's happened, I just thought. . ."

"What? What did you think?"

"I thought you. . .you know."

"I know what?" I asked. "I don't know what you're talking about, Chrissie, be clear."

"I thought you were. . ."

Trying to discern her thoughts, I asked, "What? Did you think I was dead?"

"No. I didn't think you were dead, because if you had died I would have heard from your friends." She was still sobbing and the words were tumbling out at full speed. "But then, when I didn't hear from any of them, I figured they were with you. You *do* know what I'm talking about,

Mom. You know. . .what you're *always* talking about," she said, her voice gaining more composure.

By now, what she meant was beginning to dawn on me. She was referring to the Rapture. The grin began to spread across my face and, laughing, I said, "Aha! So you *do* believe it! Ha, ha, ha on you. All this time that you've been fighting me and not wanting to hear about it, all the time you believed it."

"No, I didn't," she insisted. I could tell from her voice she was beginning to see the humor in this as well. "It's just that when I didn't hear from you I thought you were gone. You know, I mean dead. Then, when none of your friends called me about you I figured *they* were gone, too, and it was all true. That whole stupid thing."

"Well, it's obvious you don't really think it's so stupid after all, because you believed it. And I have one more 'ha-ha-ha' on you, you really love me a lot more than you think." We both laughed, but then she began scolding me for not having called sooner.

Although I have to admit it really *was* extremely inconsiderate on my part, God used this situation to open a door of communication between us. From time to time Christine calls me and says things like, "Mom, I need to talk to you about something because I need your advice. I need somebody who is *grounded*. I mean, you're the only person I know who has a foundation that is strong enough to build a life response on." This is one of those proofs that we should not look to *give* a sermon, we should be one. She had witnessed that my life was built upon the Rock, Jesus Christ. She saw that it is He Who has strengthened me through every trial.

In a recent conversation, Christine said to me, "When I think about all the ridicule you took from this family, I think it's so great that you stuck to your guns. When I think of all you have been through in your life, Mom, you still continued to love God and have faith in Him. That's what's kept you going. It's so wonderful. And I'm so very proud of you. I tell everyone about you. I say you're my best friend and I tell them you're like an old Timex watch. You take a licking, but you keep on ticking. You know, Mom, you're really my hero." Hearing those words was like music to my ears. They were a long time in coming, and I get choked up because after years and years of praying, it finally happened. Be encouraged. Never give up.

Proverbs 31:28 talks about the ideal woman and says, "Her children rise up and call her blessed." I think that's pretty much what Chrissie said, don't you agree? She may have used different words but I believe that's really what she was saying to me. Yep, I believe it. I really do. . .I think.

Honest to God. . .

Search me, O God, and know my heart; test me and know
my anxious thoughts. See if there is any offensive way
in me, and lead me in the way everlasting.
—Psalm 139:23, 24 (NIV)

*I*understand you lost a daughter a few years ago, Carole.
Would you mind talking about that with us?" the em-
cee asked.

"No, of course not," I responded. "It is almost three
years since my daughter, J. . ." I tried to say Jacqueline's
name, but I couldn't. My throat tightened, my voice caught,
and my eyes welled up with tears. I thought, *Come on,
Carole, control. Control! What's with you? You've talked about
her so many times. What's going on?*

It was 1995 and I was a guest speaker on Trinity Broad-
casting Network's Praise The Lord television talk show. I
had been on their program three times before, so I was perfectly at ease. Now, here I was on a live television show in
front of possibly thousands of people and I had choked up.
The tears rolled slowly down my face as I forced myself to
continue talking and although the words came out a little
strained, I managed to get through the interview.

Something was happening inside of me. I had no idea
what it was, but I felt as though I was beginning to come
apart emotionally. This was not normal for me because I
was always so strong. What's more, it all had to do with
Jacqueline. Every time I thought about her, I choked up.
The very mention of her name brought tears and I couldn't
talk about her to anyone without sobbing. I asked the Lord,
"Why, God? Why the incredible sadness? And why is it

happening now, three years later? What's going on with me? The pain is so incredible and I don't know what to do with it. I keep praying and asking You to take it from me, but You don't. Why?" He never answered, but I knew He had His reasons.

Just like a butterfly coming out of a cocoon, sometimes God has to let us struggle. I read somewhere that if you were to split open a cocoon to let the butterfly out, it would never take flight. It needs the struggle to build up strength in the muscles of its wings to enable it to fly. I believe that every time I asked the Lord, "God, why aren't You helping me?" all the while He must have been saying, "I *am* helping you by keeping My hands off you."

There were so many times in my life I had used the expression, "honest to God," and this was one time I not only had to be honest with Him, but I had to be honest with myself as well. Sometimes we know exactly what it is we are feeling. I didn't. Oh, I knew I was grieving, but I needed to know why; and there was something else there, something deeper. Torment. I kept turning things over in my mind in an attempt to analyze my feelings. *Am I angry with God?* I asked myself, only to quickly respond, *No. Of course I'm not angry with Him.* However, several weeks passed until I finally had to acknowledge that although I was not *angry* with God, I *was* disappointed in Him. I had come to grips with the fact that the way it ended for Jackie was not at all the way I had wanted it to end.

The reality was that I was *terribly* disappointed. Jesus told us in John 8:32 that we would know the truth and it would set us free. I thought, *Lord, no truth can set me free unless it becomes truth to me, personally. I don't understand, Jesus. If I have already acknowledged the source of my pain, then why aren't I being set free? Your love is already foundational in my life, so why am I having such a problem? Why can't I let this thing go?* Nothing changed. In every other area of my life I was functioning well, but the sadness over Jackie was still overwhelming. I could neither pray nor praise it away.

My pastor's wife said to me one day when I was sharing with her, "I don't think there is anything you can do about the pain, except to let yourself feel it. It's a part of the healing process. You never truly permitted yourself to mourn Jackie, and it's time you did." My tears were beginning to flow as she continued. "God is mercifully letting you go through it at this time because He knows now you are strong enough to bear it. As for your feelings of disappointment with God, I can't help you. You are going to have to go directly to the Lord with that." As usual, she was so right.

The Bible teaches that the two main functions of the Holy Spirit are to shed the love of God abroad in our hearts and to lead and guide us in all truth. How I desperately needed to know the truth of what was going on inside of me. There would be no freedom unless that happened. Only the Holy Spirit could do it because it was not something I could do for myself. Try as I might, I couldn't. It had to be His work, not mine, and it had to be in His good and perfect time.

As I have so many other times throughout my life, once more I asked God the question, "What else is happening here besides what's happening here?" Somehow, I knew that despite my awareness of an emotional problem, there was something that still needed to be exposed. With everything I had in me I prayed those verses in Psalm 139 and asked Him to search me and uncover any hidden sin. I knew I could trust Him because His mercy is above all His works.

It was another one of those times when I found it necessary to look back in order to validate where I was. Thoughts of Jacqueline's death or the mention of her name were the catalysts that brought on the terrible grief, so this is where I began.

Initially, I was so grateful to God for having taken Jackie Home and for delivering her out of the horrible lifestyle she was living, that I didn't really mourn her. Watching her go through the prolonged pain and suffering had brought a sense of relief when she finally died. For her, the agony was over. I had comforted myself with the fact that in the end she had been reconciled to God and to us, she was in His presence, and some day I would see her again. I knew all of that in my head, but in my heart the pain was still unbearable. Why? I still needed to know.

The Holy Spirit answered my prayer and began to gently lead me in analyzing my thoughts. Slowly I realized that my disappointment was because I had never given up hope for one moment that God would restore Jacqueline and that she would some day resume her rightful place as the mother of her little girl. Then I had to go one step further and ask, "What are the feelings behind my disappointment?" True to my tenacious nature, I pressed in until the Holy Spirit showed me that behind the disappointment was the feeling that somewhere along the way I could have done a better job. I would have made a happier ending to this scenario than God had made.

As I continued to ponder these matters week after week, I knew I had to dig beneath the many layers of my emotional disguises. Finally, one day, deeply grieved in my spirit, I saw that behind the disappointment and my feeling that I could have done a better job, was the sin of pride. Oh, it had been so very well hidden and so very well camouflaged, but it was there nonetheless. Underneath the permissible grief, there it lurked, sinister and deadly.

Make no mistake; the devil is a crafty one. His whole mission is to first destroy our faith in God and then to destroy us. I don't think it was a coincidence that less than six months after Jacqueline's death I had my second bout with cancer and almost lost my life. The enemy knows there is something about the grief of losing a child that seems to make a permanent dent in our armor that no amount of polishing can quite take away. He knew my weakness, as he does with everyone else, and he used this situation to attack me in my vulnerability. He always seems to know just where there is a breach in our armor and that is where he shoots his arrows of doubt and unbelief. His target was to get me to lose my faith in the goodness of God.

I have heard many Christians give wonderful testimonies of mighty deliverances from drugs, alcohol, or promiscuity, but when I asked Jesus into my heart, I didn't need to be delivered from any of them. No, there was something else, something far worse from which I needed to be delivered. It was the pride of being me, of my self-sufficiency and my accomplishments. It began way back in my childhood. Every time I was called some terrible name, my determination to "show them" and make something of myself had increased. Although there is nothing wrong with that, the seeds of pride were sown and watered by every goal I achieved because I gave the credit to myself and not to God.

At the time, I didn't know Him. Therefore, I had no real sense as to the true Source of my strength, my intelligence, my tenacity, or my life, for that matter. My belief system regarding myself was already damaged, so the emphasis was not on who I was, but on what I did and how well I did it. Consequently, I was an over-achiever and excelled in almost everything I did, because the pride I took in my achievements was the only thing that enabled me to feel good about myself. Justifiable? Yes. However, it was also the source of a very deep-rooted stronghold of pride. It makes me smile to think how God has a way of knocking people down off their high horse. Paul, in the Bible, was not alone.

Actually, God's work in this area had begun many years before. You might recall the chapter about my daughter, Laura, in which I wrote that her illness gave me the first inkling that I was not in control of anything. I remember watching her one day when she was in the last stages of her losing battle with a brain tumor. I was thinking, *None of this is her fault or her doing. She didn't ask for it. She did nothing to cause it. It could have happened to anyone.* . .Suddenly, the thought hit me and I said out loud, "This could have been *me!* It's true! I could have been Laura!" Now the thoughts began racing through my head. *She has no control over what's happening to her and neither do I. All her abilities have been taken away. They were given to her at first, but now they're gone.* Then came the dawn as I continued, *By the same token, my mind, my talents, or my intelligence have nothing to do with me, either. I did nothing to earn them or give them to myself. They were given to me! By God! Everything I have was given to me by Him.* What a humbling moment of truth!

Eventually I came to the point where I had to put my sadness and pain on the altar. Then I had to put my sins on the altar as well. The ax had to be laid to the root. I shuddered under the conviction that my feeling of disappointment in God was nothing more than a well-disguised sin of pride! I went into a time of true repentance and surrendered both my reasons and my rights. I cried and told God how sorry I was and asked Him to forgive me, and I know He did. His Word says, "If we confess our sins, He is faithful and just to forgive us our sins, and cleanse us from all unrighteousness." (1 John 1:9). What a comfort that is.

God had done a mighty work and yet, there was still one more necessary step. That was dealing with my unforgiveness. Sometimes we harbor unforgiveness in our hearts, and we are loath to even acknowledge its presence. As odd as it may seem to some, I knew I had to forgive God. Forgive God? Did He do something *wrong?* Was He *guilty* of something? No, of course not. Although He was guiltless, Jacqueline's death had deeply wounded my heart, and I had to forgive in order to allow the poison to drain from the wound. I humbled myself once more and cried, "Oh God, please forgive me for what I am saying. You don't need my forgiveness, but *I* need to forgive You. I know You didn't do anything wrong, but somewhere deep in my heart I held You responsible. *I was wrong.* Please forgive me, Lord, for having held on to that sin for so long. I now release all my pain to You, Father." As I prayed, I felt as though spiritual chains fell from my heart, and the torment lifted. I was set free at last.

The Bible tells us in Matthew 5:4, "Blessed are they that mourn, for they shall be comforted." It is so true. Grieving is part of a necessary process, and Jesus was telling us that unless we acknowledge the pain and allow ourselves to mourn our losses, we will not be comforted. I thank God I was able to go through that process, because the comfort did come.

Does this mean I never again cried about Jacqueline? Of course not. I still do sometimes when I miss her. Until I see her once again, I keep looking to Jesus and am able to say to Him, "My Jesus, You are so merciful and good. You are all grace, mercy, and love bound together in a single Person. I love You, Lord. I really do—honest to God!"

The Third Victory

But thanks be to God which giveth us the victory through our Lord Jesus Christ.
—1 Corinthians 15:57

*I*waited patiently as the technician removed the respirator tube from my throat, and I looked into the eyes of my doctor standing nearby. "How are you?" he asked. "Can you talk? Or is your throat too sore?"

"No, I can talk," I answered. "But *you tell me*, Doctor Calio, how am I?" He shook his head. I said, "Oh, come on. Don't just shake your head like that. Tell me. How bad was it?"

He shook his head once again and said, "Massive."

"How massive?"

"The surgeon had to remove the entire right lobe of your liver, the gall bladder, and another mass in the chest cavity that was imbedded in the diaphragm. That's why you needed the respirator."

"Am I going to make it this time?" I asked.

He responded, "I don't know. It all depends on if your body can handle all the trauma and, of course, a lot depends on your attitude."

My thoughts went back over the last five days since the surgery. I had drifted in and out of consciousness as the morphine drip floated my brain from reality into a fog of nothingness. How I hated that morphine. Yes, it subdued the pain, but it also caused a nightmare of confusion and the feeling of being totally disconnected from everything. Yet, from time to time little glimpses of reality had been brought into focus.

I could remember Christine standing at my bedside talking to me and crying very hard. Another time I saw this same doctor sitting in a chair next to my bed with his head bowed. He was holding my hand up to his face, and I could feel his lips moving against my fingers in prayer. One day I was able to summon enough consciousness to remember that Heather was now twelve years old—old enough to go white water rafting. I had promised her this year she could come with the group. I was also dimly aware of blood transfusions, tubes everywhere, a machine doing the breathing for me and, from time to time, wondering if I was going to die. I remember asking God, "What if I don't make it this time? If I die, I won't be able to keep my promise to Heather. And I've never broken a promise to her. . ."

My thoughts were interrupted by the doctor, "We'll just have to wait and see what happens," he was saying.

Still thinking about Heather, I asked, "Am I going to be able to go white water rafting this June?"

He just threw up his hands and said, "I can't believe this woman. You've had a massive amount of surgery and you just had a respirator tube taken out of your throat, and you're worrying about *white water rafting?*" Then, shaking his head, he said, "Well, if you're thinking about rafting, you're going to make it." We both smiled.

"I saw you praying for me here one day," I said, changing the subject.

He said, "Yes, well, I have a lot of patients, but you've really gotten to me." He meant it. Dr. Anthony Calio is not only one of the most loved and respected doctors in the profession but a genuinely nice person. We often talked about God together, and I found he already had a close relationship with the Lord.

Over the last eleven years I have had ten surgeries. Three were major operations because of cancer and the others were for removal of different tumors in various parts of my body which, thank God, were all benign. This gave me many opportunities to witness to my doctors and I took advantage of every one. We not only have a great rapport with one another, but I believe a genuine friendship and a kind of love have developed.

When the latest MRI had shown that the lesion on my liver had tripled in size since the previous test, there was no doubt that the situation was serious. When my doctor saw the look of concern on my face, he asked, "Carole, what do you always say to me?"

"I don't know, Doctor. What do I always say to you?" I answered.

He said, "You always say to me, 'God is good.'" I never realized until then that I do say it often.

"And, Carole," he added, "God is *still* good." I agreed. Then he said, "The way God has brought you through before, He will do the same for you this time." My heart skipped a beat when he added, "I will pray for you." I never thought that a doctor would actually pray for a patient, but he did. Not only he, but some of his office workers actually sent messages saying they were also praying for me. God *is* good—all the time!

About a week after the surgery, I had spent an agonizing night crying out to the Lord. The pain was almost unbearable and the doctors were suspecting an abdominal abscess. Wave after wave of pain swept through me, and in desperation I cried out to Jesus, "Lord, I don't understand. How can You allow me to go through this? I try to glorify You in all that I do and in all things. But how. . .? How does this bring You glory? No one in the entire world knows the pain I'm going through, except You and I. So how does this glorify You? I don't know what to think anymore. Was the pain of the surgery not enough? Why this too? I know You love me, but I don't understand. I feel so alone, so forsaken."

It was still very early in the morning, and as I lay there crying, the telephone rang. It was my pastor's wife. "Carole," she said, "what's going on with you? The Lord put you on my heart and I haven't been able to sleep all night."

I cried and told her about the pain and all that had been going through my mind, and ended with, "I feel so forsaken."

She asked, "Carole, when Jesus was being buffeted and bruised, spat upon, and had His beard yanked out of His face, had His Father forsaken Him?"

"No," I answered.

"Neither has He forsaken you," she said. She continued, "When He hung on the cross and He cried out, 'My God, My God why hast Thou forsaken Me?' had His Father actually forsaken Him?"

"No," I repeated.

"And neither has He forsaken you. He knows about every pain, every tear, every cry of your heart and, although I don't understand it any more than you do why you have to go through this, the Father does. Somehow, in some way, He will bring it to glory. Maybe not the way we think it will be done, but according to His perfect, infinitely wise and loving will."

Those words were all I needed. They put me right back on track. It was true. He *did* know what I was going through. The fact that He had put me on her heart and had prompted her to call was simply to show me that, indeed, He had not forsaken me. Through all the pain that followed, I was able to rest in Him and continue to praise God. Like Job in the Bible, I kept repeating, "Though He slay me, yet will I trust in Him." (Job 13:15a).

With each passing day one complication after another set in. One day I reminded Jesus, "Your Word says You never give us more than we can handle and You always make a way out for us. Well, I'm holding You to it, Lord. I hope You don't think I'm being impertinent and that You will indulge me, but I've just about had it. And I hope You're smiling. I'm not, but I hope You are."

Although I was attempting to employ my old coping mechanism of making jokes, the reality was that my condition was quite serious. It was not a time for heroism, so I unashamedly reached out to the Body of Christ. With every new circumstance, the call went forth to the brethren for increased prayer. They all responded so faithfully with praise, supplication, and thanksgiving, that healing took place every time. With every attack came an even greater victory. Glory to God, we *are* more than conquerors!

I spent sixteen days in the hospital and the Holy Spirit was at work during that entire time. Aside from my own personal victories, His first mighty work was done through Heather. My friends, Eileen and Mike, had kept Heather at their house from before the surgery, and this was the first time she was seeing me in three weeks. She was so happy that she wept, and then ever so carefully climbed alongside me on the bed and laid her cheek against mine. I could feel the warmth of her tears against my skin as we held each other in silence.

At the time there were two doctors talking to my roommate, Helen, about some surgical procedure they were going to perform the next day. When the aide brought in my supper tray, Heather got up and busied herself preparing my tea and buttering my bread. She was smiling and so happy to be helping me that one of the doctors turned as he was leaving the room and said, "You know, you are a very special young lady. I've been watching you, and there aren't very many young girls your age who have a servant's heart, but you do."

I cannot help feeling he must have been a Christian, because the world doesn't see or acknowledge things like that. Heather just beamed. With that, the woman said, "I've noticed what a special little girl you are, too."

Heather smiled and then asked her, "Is there something I can do for you?"

The woman answered, "Well, yes, there is. I would like you to say a prayer for me that God would heal me." Eileen's eyes met mine and widened with wonder, aware that a move of the Holy Spirit was taking place. Heather beamed once more and said she would love to do that for her. She walked over to her bed and laid her hand against the woman's forehead, but then she hesitated for a moment.

She said to the woman, "I can say a prayer for your healing, but I think there's something you need to do first. Have you ever given your heart to Jesus?"

Helen said, "No." At first, Eileen and I didn't know whether to laugh or cry. We were doing a little bit of both.

Heather continued, "Well, it's just that you have to tell Jesus that you are sorry for your sins, and that you know He died to pay the price so that you don't have to go to hell when you die. Then you ask Him to come into your heart and live there. Would you like to do that?"

The woman said she would, and Heather proceeded to lead her step by step through the prayer. With God, it's never too early and it's never too late. After the woman invited Jesus into her heart, eleven-year-old Heather simply laid her hand on the forehead of this eighty-seven-year-old woman and said, "Father, this is your child, I ask that You would please heal her in the name of Jesus. Thank You, Lord. Amen." Eileen and I were no longer laughing.

I had no idea that Heather was so well versed in all the aspects of Jesus' redemptive work on the Cross. Oh, how important it is to explain the things of God to little children. I've been accused by some of teaching her too much, that it's too much for little minds to grasp, but it gets in. Children are like sponges, soaking up the Living Water. We plant the seeds, but the Holy Spirit gives the increase, and oh, the fruit it bears.

Two days later Helen went Home to be with the Lord. The entire night before she died she was in agony. I passed the hours crying, praying, and talking about Jesus to the two night nurses who stayed in the room. They prayed the prayer of salvation with me and before they went off duty, they brought in the head nurse and one other nurse and they, too, gave their lives to the Lord. Before I left the hospital there were twelve names added to the Lamb's Book of Life. Glory!

When I called Heather with the news that Helen died, at first she wept. Then she said, "But Grandma, I prayed for her to be healed. Then, again, she *is* healed now, isn't she, Grandma." How true are the words, "Oh death, where is thy sting, Oh grave, where is thy victory?" (1 Corinthians 15:55). The victory is not in the circumstances of our lives, but in the full and finished work of Jesus Christ on the Cross. I have no idea why He has allowed me to come through so many battles and has kept me alive. Nevertheless, I'm so grateful that He has healed me and given me the privilege to continue serving Him. This battle was a rough one but, once more, through Jesus the victory was mine.

Keep on Keeping On

And let us not be weary in well doing: for in due time
we shall reap, if we faint not.

—Galatians 6:9

*I*n the months preceding my last major surgery in 1997,
the Holy Spirit began moving mightily in the lives of
the people around me—strangers, as well as long-time
friends. It was as though all the years of intercessory prayer
was finally paying off. Wherever I went, God presented
golden opportunities for me to pray people into the Kingdom.

I have a very dear friend, Kay, whom I have known for
over forty years. In fact, we were in each other's wedding
parties. Over the years, our families often vacationed together, along with other long-time friends. Those were always wonderful, laughter-filled vacations as we all ribbed
one another good-naturedly. Kay's husband, Harry, especially enjoyed teasing and poking fun at me, sometimes
gently and sometimes not so gently. I often reminded him
of the very first time we met when he turned to Kay and
said, "Aww, Kathleen, she's not as much of a dog as you
said she was."

Then I would say to him in mock anger, "And it's been
down hill ever since!" Occasionally I would say, "Harry,
some day you are going to be sorry for all the mean things
you've said, and you are going to admit that underneath it
all, you really love me." Then we would laugh and give one
another a hug.

As the years passed and my life and my walk with the
Lord got more serious, we drifted apart and didn't see as

much of each other. However, whenever I picked up the telephone to call Kay, it was as though we had only spoken the day before. That's how it is with friends. Eventually the time came when Kay prayed with me and accepted Jesus, but no matter what I said to Harry, he would just smile and turn away. One day I even wept while urging him to ask Jesus into his heart, but it didn't matter. He was not interested.

The urgency to witness to my friends had been mounting over the last year, and now it seemed to override all my timidity. One week prior to my surgery, I knew my condition was serious. This was possibly a life or death situation, and I needed to touch base with all my close friends, just in case the Lord decided to take me Home. When I called, Kay was suffering from a virus and was upstairs in bed, so I talked with Harry.

Near the end of our conversation I repeated how I had been praying for him and hoped with all my heart that some day he would come to accept Jesus as Lord. I began to cry, and Harry said, "I tell you what, Carole, when you come out of the hospital and everything is all right, I'll come over some afternoon and you can pray with me then."

Timidly, I suggested, "We can pray right now, Harry."

"Yes, we can," he answered. My heart skipped a beat. Did he mean what I thought he meant?

"Do you want to?" I asked.

"Yes, I do," he answered quietly. And so, we prayed. By the time we finished, I was so ecstatic I was blubbering all over the place. Yet, somewhere in the back of my mind was a small area of concern. I wondered whether Harry had prayed because he wanted to or that he felt sorry for me because I was crying. Even worse, maybe he had prayed just to get me off his back.

One week later, the day before the surgery, Harry called my house. In forty years, he had never once called. This was a first. We talked for less than two minutes, but I could make no sense at all of the conversation.

Two or three times he repeated himself. "I know you're going in the hospital tomorrow," he said, "so I just called to ask how you are feeling." Each time I repeated my answer, saying I was feeling fine. Then, abruptly, he said good-bye and hung up. I sat there scratching my head, wondering what that call was all about.

While I was still reflecting on it, the phone rang once again. It was Harry. "Carole," he said, "I really called before to tell you something, but I never said it. Listen, I just want to say thank you for leading me to Jesus. I can't tell you what it's done in my life. I've been reading my Bible every day, and I want to thank you for never giving up on me. When I think of all the guff you took over the years and you never gave up on me. . ." At that point, he choked up. I was already crying, but we continued laughing and talking through our emotions. Then he added, "And there's one more thing I have to tell you. You were right. I *do* love you." Now we both laughed with the joy of the Lord.

We serve a mighty God. So often in our lives we are tempted to simply give up. Whether it is in some other area of difficulty or praying for our friends and loved ones, if we keep on believing in Him, He gives us the ability to keep on keeping on.

A "God Thing"

Has not God chosen those who are poor in the eyes of
the world...to inherit the kingdom He promised...?
—James 2:5 (NIV)

*A*bout a month after I came home from the hospital,
two friends drove me to a local Christian bookstore
to do some shopping. We walked around and
shopped for awhile, but soon I got very tired. I was still
weak from the surgery and felt a little shaky, so I said I
would go outside and sit on the steps to wait for them.
There was a railing dividing the steps outside, and as I
walked down the stairs and sat down, an old man came
walking by. This was not an ordinary man, but someone
who would qualify to be called a street person. He was un-
washed, unshaved, his clothes were dirty and wrinkled, and
the smell wafting from his person made me hold my breath
and look away. As he was passing, he turned his head and
stared at me. Then he turned around, walked a few steps
back, and sat down on the other side of the railing. I wasn't
too happy because, not only was his body odor overwhelming, but he was smoking a cigarette and blowing the smoke
in my face.

At this point, I was annoyed. After the first time he ex-
haled and coughed in my direction, I looked directly at him
and then turned my head away. Once more he puffed on
his cigarette, blew out the smoke and coughed. Now, I was
really annoyed. I thought, *Do I need this? Here I am fighting
for my life and I have to have this person polluting my lungs
with his cigarette smoke.* This time, I definitely gave him a
dirty look.

He looked back and said, "I'm dyin', ya' know."

I thought, *You're not the only one. If the doctors are right, I'm dying too. I've already used up two of the four months they gave me to live.* I thought it, but I didn't want to say those words because I was trying to only speak life into my situation. I just stared at him and didn't answer.

He said, "No, really! Doctor says I'm a dyin' man. My lungs are shot and I'm gonna die." Part of me wanted to start giving him a sermon about smoking, but then I thought, *What's the point of that? What good would it do?*

I turned from him again, when suddenly the thought flashed across my mind, *He says he's dying. If he doesn't know Jesus and he dies, then he's going to hell.* I looked back in his direction and asked, "Where are you going when you die?"

He said, "What?"

Matter-of-factly I repeated the question, "You said you were dying, so I'm asking you, where are you going when you die?"

The man looked slightly puzzled for a minute and then said, "Uh, I guess I'm goin' to the undertaker."

"No," I answered, "that's where your *body* is going, but where are *you* going when you die?"

Now he was really puzzled and thought for several minutes before he answered, "Oh *that!* Oh, straight down!" he said, motioning and pointing his thumb toward the ground. "Yep, straight down. I was in the navy for twenty-six years. And after the life I've lived? I ain't goin' nowhere but straight down." If you can believe it, he was actually chuckling as he answered me.

I hope you understand that although mercy is not my number-one motivational gift, seeing people come to Jesus *is.* So, at that point, I stood up and walked around the railing to face him. I looked straight into his eyes and gently asked, "Did anyone ever tell you that there was a man called

Jesus Christ Who was the Son of God, and He came down from heaven to die on a cross to pay the price for all your sins, so that when *you* die you don't have to go '*straight down*'?"

He was no longer laughing. He looked deep into my eyes and I saw a little line of tears well up. I knew this was a "God thing." I began to outline God's wonderful plan of salvation, and after ten minutes or so I asked him, "Would you like to pray with me now to receive Jesus as your Savior and Lord?"

Meekly, he said he would, so I took his hands in mine and we began to pray. You must know this really *was* a "God thing" because only the Holy Spirit enabled me to stand two feet away from him without gagging. But I did! The funny thing is that just as we began to pray, my two friends came walking out of the store. When they saw me standing there holding hands with this man, the expression on their faces was nothing less than comical. I looked up at them and said, "Pray!" And they did.

As we concluded the prayer, I actually gave him a hug. It was amazing; the joy was so visible that as he walked away there was a new spring to his step. He suddenly turned back to me and said, "Wow. I can't wait to go back to the boarding house. My landlady is a Christian and she's been praying for me for over two years to get saved. Wait 'till I tell her what happened."

What an encouragement this is for those of us who pray and witness to people. Although we may not always see the results, we never know who else will come along and complete the work that began with our prayers. I wonder how many times there are wonderful opportunities all around us and we are completely oblivious to them? For years, I have prayed for "holy boldness" to be able to speak to people about what Jesus has done, and God has given it to me. I'm not obnoxious about it, but neither am I intimidated by my surroundings or by the person's status in life. It doesn't matter to me if they own the finest piece of real estate, because if they don't have a place reserved for them in glory, they have nothing. Nor does it matter if they have all kinds of initials after their name. If their name isn't written down in the Lamb's Book of Life, again it means nothing.

When I see people walking aimlessly through life, my heart aches for them to have what I have—that hope and promise of eternal joy in the presence of God. No matter where I am it seems that He opens the door, enabling me to pray one more person into the Kingdom. Laughingly, I tell people that if I ever fell into a manhole, there would be somebody else in there that God wanted to get saved.

What about you, dear reader? Have you felt that call to do His work? Pray for it. The Word says it is God's will that none should perish, and you never know when He will do a "God thing" in *your* life.

"I Made It!" - Cards Number 5–7

Even when I am old and gray-headed, O God, forsake me not, [but keep me alive] until I have declared Your mighty strength to [this] generation, and Your might and power to all that are to come.

—Psalm 71:18 (AMP)

"I Made It!" — Card #5

June 17, 1998

Hi there,

Well, it's that time again. Another year has gone by and I've made it to the big *"Five."* All things being considered, and giving thanks and praise to God, I am not only still alive but I'm doing very well—albeit with a few less body parts than I started off with five years ago. It just goes to show how we can make do with less when we have to.

As you already know, in my relationship with God I am always saying how wonderful He is. And, of course, He is. But I ask you, with all I've had removed on the inside, wouldn't you think I would be skinny on the outside? Is He fair?—only kidding. Actually, I've never been so pleased at being overweight as I am now. In fact, I've never been so pleased at almost everything in life as I am now.

This past weekend I did my yearly white water rafting trip down the Lehigh Valley Gorge with fifty other friends, including my granddaughter, Heather, who is now twelve-and-a-half years old. What a trip!

I deliberately chose the day they were having a dam release to make it more exciting. Strangely enough, I find more than a few similarities between these rafting trips and life. It's true.

The instructions for navigating the Lehigh are really not so different from some of the circumstances and rules for getting through life. How so, you ask? I'll tell you. Each turn and bend in the sixteen-mile run down the River brings new vistas of beauty as God's creativity and glory reveals itself. At the same time, you have to learn to maneuver over and around thousands of rocks and boulders. Some of them you can see, but others are submerged just beneath the surface of the water. In fact, it is the water moving over and around those rocks that creates the rapids, and the turmoil is a warning that there is something there that needs to be dealt with.

Before the trip even begins, the instructor says that if we listen up and follow the safety rules, we will get much more enjoyment from the trip. (Something like the "Thou Shalt" or "Thou Shalt Not's" of life.) We are warned that while going down the river we could get bumped, bruised, or even tossed out of the raft, and we are told what to do if that should happen. The challenge of shooting the rapids is both scary and exhilarating and, once you get past them, nothing compares with the feeling you get at having come through victoriously.

Once in a while, though, you come up against some huge rocks that stick up out of the water some eight or ten feet. Due to the force of the current, there are times when collision is inevitable. That's when the real similarity with life comes in.

When there is no way of avoiding a collision, we are taught to go against our natural instincts to pull away and are told that, just before the impact, we must lean into and against the rock. The reason for this is that if all the weight is on the side away from the contact point, the force of the water underneath the raft will cause the lighter side of the raft to rise up against the face of the rock, causing the whole thing to capsize. However, when you lean forward and pit yourself against the rock, it may hurt, but you bounce right off it. Believe me, when you see that rock looming up in front of you and you know you are about to collide, it takes a lot of discipline to follow the instructions, but they work! You know, that's what I have learned to do with my unavoidable "collisions" in life. The only difference is that instead of leaning into "a" rock, I have learned to lean into "The" Rock—the Lord Jesus Christ.

Just like the actual river, in between the rapids you come to the eddies. But even in the "calms" of this past year, God has kept me busy. I am still writing and trying to get my latest book published, (the first one has now topped 47,000 copies in circulation) and I have a couple of ideas for a third book and several articles. In between I've been busy being a "mommy" to Heather, doing speaking engagements, conducting seminars as well as still teaching an adult Bible study at home and the teens in our church on Sundays.

Anyway, that is what has been going on with me. How about you? Where have you gone and what have you done this year? Has it all been "smooth sailing?" Or have there been some rocks in your river? Sometimes the rocks in life can be as big as mountains, but God always makes a way. There are some lines from a song that I think about from time to time. They say that whether you have a mountain in your life that is blocking your path, or a river you think is uncrossable, God specializes in impossible tasks and He can do what no one else can do.

I believe that it is no accident we have been a part of each other's life, however minuscule that part might be. God has used each of you to help add to both the quantity and the quality of my life, and for that I am so grateful. I pray you don't mind these yearly little "sermonettes" from me and that they cause you to ponder where you are going to be at the end of your trip down the river of life. I've only shared this because it is my hope that when you come up against the inevitable rocks or impacts in your life that you, too, will remember to lean into the Rock.

In closing, I send you my prayer for God's choicest blessings on you and yours at the level of your deepest needs. I look forward to writing to you again next year and that the news will continue to be good. Just remember that God loves you and, in His name, so do I.

God bless,

Carole

"I Made It!" — Card #6

June 15, 1999

Hello again,

Can you imagine? Another year has passed and we're up to number six. To be honest, as time has passed and with each day of good health, I am in awe and filled with such incredible thanksgiving that I've made it thus far. I'm convinced that part of my amazing endurance has been an attitude of gratitude for every day and moment of my life.

There is really so very much that I have to be thankful for. First of all for the Lord, Himself, Who is the Strength of my life. Then all the other wonderful people—my daughter Chris, and, of course, my lovely little granddaughter, Heather, who is graduating from junior high school. She's really not so little anymore, she is almost as tall as I am now. Not that that is such an accomplishment, seeing as I am only 4'10,' but it is so funny for me to be at eye level with her. I also have some really wonderful friends who are truly a blessing.

Just so that you know, not only am I still alive, but I'm alive and still kicking. Last weekend we went on our yearly white water rafting jaunt down the Lehigh River and, as usual, it was a blast. I swear that I must laugh myself into six months more of good health with each trip. Actually, I'm blessed with a good sense of humor and I've learned to laugh a lot, despite all the ups and downs of life.

You know, when I bragged to you six years ago that I was going to send you a card every year on the anniversary of my surgery, I was so determined that with God's help I was going to make it. I realize that my attitude and changing my diet certainly helped but, in actuality, it has really all been up to Him. It's only by His grace and mercy that I'm still teaching, conducting seminars, writing, cooking, cleaning, gardening, keeping up with Heather, and having fun.

Do I get tired? You'd better believe it. After all, I am almost sixty-four years old. But it sure makes for a good night's sleep. And every morning I'm so glad to be alive that I can't wait to see what the Lord is going to do in my life and the lives of those around me that day.

You know, there was a time when I used to complain because I had to get up during the night to use the bathroom and it disturbed my sleep. Now, I'm so grateful that I have legs I can walk on and that my body parts know enough to wake me up because there's something I have to do—and that I can do it—that I no longer complain about anything.

This is what getting struck with cancer did for me. I've learned to look at the myriad of blessings that have come forth as a result. For one thing, I've realized how very tenuous is this thing we call life, and I've gotten a real appreciation for all that it entails. Sure, I've had pain and more surgery, but I'm still here to talk about it. And life has certainly not been without its heartache—in the past year I lost both my mother and my sister. Still, God has kept me and allowed me to keep going.

So many times when we look at the sorrows of life we see only the hard, ugly coverings. However, I have learned to look beneath the coverings to find the blessings. When I took the time to look is when I found a divine gift, supremely crafted and wrought by Loving Hands. I look forward to heaven, but I've found that there's a little bit of heaven in everything here on earth. And, if we grasp it, within our reach is joy.

Once more, I cannot end without touching on the subject that is the main thrust and desire of my life. That is, that you should come to know Jesus as your Lord and Savior. Whatever the situations are in your own life, whether joyous or sad, I beg you to look and reach out for the divine gift that lies behind it. Better still, reach out for the Giver of that gift and receive what He purchased for you at the Cross.

Until next year, then, I raise a prayer that you and yours are well, and for blessings at the level of your deepest needs.

God bless,

Carole

"I Made It!" — Card #7

June 17, 2000

Well, hello there,

As you can see, this is the big #7—seven whole years that I can still write and say, "I made it!" Of course, I wouldn't even have one more breath, let alone one more day, if it weren't all by the grace of God.

This past year was certainly not without its share

of joy, sadness, challenges, setbacks, and victories. Speaking of challenges, you know that every June we go white water rafting. Well, last year I went down a good portion of the river without the raft and actually had to be rescued. It was scary, because when I came up for air the third time and swallowed a lung-full of water, I thought that maybe my time had run out. But, (big smile) God pulled me through once more. And, yes, we're going again this year—in fact, this year we have seventy-eight people going on the trip.

Another episode that became an area of some concern for a while was that a new wrinkle seemed to have worked its way into the fabric of my health-life. That is, due to some repetitive symptoms, which seemed to worsen over a period of several months, there was a real possibility of a blockage in one or more of the arteries leading from the heart.

It's funny, but because God had brought me through so many years of fighting cancer, I somehow thought I was impervious to any other major health problem. Well, as some of you already know, after months of continuous shortness of breath and chest pain/pressure, while I was ministering on a weekend retreat, it all suddenly left. I believe the Lord stepped in once more and healed me, and despite tests that had shown evidence of a real problem, when I went in on Monday morning for the angiogram, there was no blockage anywhere. Not only that but, with no medical explanation, the symptoms have never returned since that day. Praise God!

This year I will hit the big sixty-five, and instead of slowing down, I'm busier than ever—especially in the area of speaking at conferences and retreats. Of course, my wonderful Heather still keeps me very busy. She's almost fifteen, taller than I am, and in high school now. Talk about challenges!

In all, I find the most important thing I have working for me is my gratitude for every single day. Most of all, I've learned to count my blessings. In that regard, I want to share something I heard that said we should always count our blessings and not our crosses; count our gains, not our losses; count our smiles, not our tears; count our courage, not our fears; count our friends, not our foes; count our joys, not our woes; count our health, not our wealth, count on God and not ourselves.

Well, I guess that's it for this year. I pray you and yours are well and that you take some time to thank, honor, and glorify God for the awesome work He has given your hands to do. Until next year, God willing, I pray blessings of health, peace, love, and joy to you all and that you come to a personal knowledge of Him.

With sincere love and respect,

Carole

One More Time

With long life will I satisfy him and show him my
salvation.

—Psalm 91:16 (NIV)

*W*ould you please tell the doctor that I'm having a
lot of pressure in my chest," I said. "I don't know
whether or not I'm having a heart attack, but I
need to talk to him." The receptionist buzzed me right
through and my doctor came on the line.

"What's going on?" he asked. I told him my symptoms
and he said, "Doesn't sound good to me. Can you get in
here right away?"

I said yes, and instead of getting a ride there, I drove to
his office.

For several months, I had been having difficulty breathing while walking up stairs or doing anything strenuous.
Recently, the same thing was happening at even the slight-
est exertion. Now, even at rest, I was not only having difficulty breathing, but I kept having a sensation that was not
quite pain, not quite burning, but more like a terrible pressure, either against my chest or coming from within. Other
times I felt a sudden pain in my back, as though someone
had punched me very hard between my shoulder blades. I
remembered that a few weeks before, a friend of mine was
told the aspirin that he took had made the difference between a major or minor heart attack. Keeping this in mind,
I began popping aspirins with every symptom, sometimes
as many as ten a day.

Until now I had put off getting medical attention, because part of me thought I was impervious to having any

real heart problems. I figured God wouldn't bring me through all that cancer and then take me out with a heart attack. Nevertheless, I was getting really concerned. Sitting there is his office, I told my doctor, "I have to feel better because tomorrow morning I'm leaving to do a retreat at the Convention Center in Atlantic City, and it's very important for me to be there."

He just smiled and said, "We'll see."

After his examination, he immediately directed me to his associate, a cardiologist, for further testing. I was strapped to all kinds of machines and various tests were done, including a stress test. However, only two minutes into the test, the cardiologist stopped the treadmill saying, "I've seen enough. The cardiogram shows there is a definite problem."

He then explained that I had all the classic symptoms pointing to one or more clogged arteries leading from the heart. When he strongly suggested that I sign myself into the hospital that very afternoon, I told him, "I can't. I'm leaving tomorrow morning for Atlantic City. I'm scheduled to speak at a Christian conference at the convention center."

He smiled and said, "You are not going anywhere except to the hospital."

"But I have to," I said. "One of the other speakers had a death in their family and I have to be there."

He replied, "Well, there may be more than one death this week if you don't listen to me. You have every symptom and very strong indication of having a blockage in one or more of the arteries leading from your heart."

After he explained the very real danger to my life, I finally agreed that after making arrangements for Heather, I would sign myself into the hospital. At that exact point, the telephone rang. The cardiologist's eyes were twinkling as he hung up and turned to me with a smile. "You must be a very special person, because that was Doctor Calio on the phone just now, and he thinks the world of you."

I responded, "It's mutual."

He continued, "He said people that do the kind of thing you do for God have a special protection around them. He said I should give you medication and let you go, only if you promise to check yourself in on Monday morning for an angiogram and a possible angioplasty." *Yes!*

Although the doctor prescribed several medications, after reading all the side effects, I thought it best not to take them. I was doing the driving, and I didn't want to have any unusual or bizarre reactions in the car. Instead, I continued taking the aspirin for the constant pressure, figuring if it had kept me comfortable so far, it would suffice for the weekend. The next day I drove the one hundred fifty miles to Atlantic City with my prayer partner.

Early on Saturday morning I awoke with enormous chest pressure and immediately took two aspirins. As we walked to the convention center from the hotel, I was terribly short of breath and several times I had to stop walking and rest. The pressure was still there, so as soon as we got inside, I popped one more aspirin for good measure. I was the first speaker of the day, and about fifteen minutes into my talk, I was aware that the pressure was slowly leaving my chest. It was the first time in weeks I could take a full, deep breath. I thought, *Wow, this time the aspirin really kicked in.* However, as the day went on, I realized that neither the pain, nor the pressure had returned.

I do approximately fifteen to twenty speaking engagements and several weekend retreats each year. During those times I never get adequate sleep, and by the end of the day I'm pretty well wiped out. As usual, toward the end of this conference, the speakers were asked to come to the front of the room. The women were told that if they needed individual ministering, they should come forward for prayer. About a dozen women walked directly over to me, and when I began to minister, something happened. Never have I experienced a surge of God's power as I did then. It felt like waves coming upon me and passing through me. It was almost palpable, almost as though I was a conduit of His love flowing through me and into them, allowing them to open up to a deeper level of His healing power.

As I prayed with each woman, one after another broke and began weeping. The breaking of which I speak is an emotional tearing down of the walls of self-protection people build around themselves so that no one else gets to know how hurt and vulnerable they really are. The Lord had never ministered through me in this way before. It is something I cannot truly describe.

On the way home I said to my friend, "I don't know what happened in there. I felt so much love and power flowing through my heart today. I bet if there was any kind of blockage in any of my arteries, it's gone!" And it was! I drove home on Saturday night and felt so alive that I was awake until 4:30 in the morning and feeling wonderful.

On Monday morning I arrived at the hospital and, prior to the test, I requested not to have a sedative added to the intravenous. The cardiologist asked me, "Are you sure you want to stay awake for this?"

"Yes, I'm sure." I said, "How many times in my life will I have the chance to see my own heart?"

He just grinned and said, "Okay." It was wonderful. I kept my eyes on the little television screen nearby in total fascination. All the while I watched the procedure, I continued to praise God for the wondrous things He does. It was fascinating to see my heart muscles working in perfect synchronization, and with each beat seeing my own blood surging out and into the arteries. Only God could have made a heart, and I thanked Him that mine was working so perfectly. The cardiologist could not believe it when the results showed no blockages anywhere. What is more, over a year has passed and none of the symptoms have ever returned. Glory!

Weeks later I felt the need to discuss this matter with my doctor. Actually, I wrote him a very long letter, parts of which I want to share with you, dear reader. That is because it contained many unanswerable questions we have all asked at one time or another. I wrote:

Dear Doctor Calio,

There is a reason why I've written you a letter instead of calling your office. Mainly because this is going to be long, and I don't think it's fair to take up so much of your time to ponder questions and answers for me while there are so many others who really need your attention. On the other hand, I needed to "talk" to you because there are unanswered questions that maybe you can answer for me. The only other Person I can ask is God, and either He has already answered me and I haven't understood Him, or He's leaving it up to me to figure out. That's usually what He does.

I think it's very possible I'm trying to determine whether I'm feeling some kind of misplaced guilt. That is because there are so many people I know of who are dying. I either know *of* them because people are always calling and asking me to pray for them, or I know *them* personally. Yet, the Lord seems to have His hand on me, keeping me alive and well. Make no mistake about it; I'm ecstatically happy that He has. It's just that I don't understand. Maybe you can help give me some explanations about what *you* think happened.

Perhaps there is a physical explanation. This is where you come in, Doctor. I do not know what causes angina. What else causes it besides blocked arteries or some other kind of heart disease? Does it come and go in spurts like this? How come it stopped before I ever began taking any medication for it? How come it never came back? I've wanted to call and ask you and the cardiologist these questions but I didn't want to take up your time. Not that either one of you wouldn't give me the time, because you are two wonderful and dedicated doctors. I am so blessed. Believe me, that's a "God thing," too, that you both are my doctors. You are extremely capable and caring, and both of you are loved and admired by your staffs—and your patients as well!

I'm feeling a real ambivalence. Partly because I have heard so many people who pray and claim miraculous healings for themselves or others and, meanwhile, two months later the person is dead. So much for the miracle! On the other hand, *something* definitely happened to me on that Saturday, and I need to talk about it. I don't want to slap God in the face by not giving Him the glory He deserves for His healing touch. It wasn't even something I was praying for. I just wanted to do for Him what He had called me to do.

I know God heals. I'm living proof of that fact. Yes, I've had people ask me, "Why has God let you go through all those operations? Why didn't He just heal you?" The answer is, "I don't know." For that matter, why did my four-year-old die of a brain tumor? Why wasn't my twenty-eight-year-old daughter healed? Why, last month, did a six-year-old I know and a mother of four die of cancer? I don't know! Why has He spared my life and kept me alive? I don't know that either. I'm just so eternally grateful that He has. I don't know why God does things the way He does. Did I not pray for my children not to die? Of course I did. God doesn't always answer our prayers the way we want them answered and I don't understand Him. But I still love Him. I only know that whatever He does, in the whole scope of things which only He can see, He does it right. Someday we will know all.

So, what do you think? Have you ever heard of a real miraculous healing? Is this one? Or is it possible that there is a very logical medical explanation and this is only a lull in the storm? I don't know these answers, but you probably have some kind of explanation. I only know that this situation reminds me of a story in the Bible about a man who was born blind. When Jesus restored his sight, he was called into the temple to refute his healing because they said Jesus was evil. He answered and said, "Whether He is a sinner or not, I don't know. One thing I do know. I was blind, but now I can see." (John 9:25) (NIV).

It's the same now with me. All I know is that I had almost continuous chest/back pain/pressure for some time and now I don't. And although there was a strong probability that there was a blocked artery, there is none. What do you think? I hope you just don't think I'm nuts but that you have some kind of answers for me. Take your time, I'm here.

Anyway, I apologize for making this such a long discourse. It has been on my heart and I just had to share it. I don't know what God is doing through all of this. I have learned to look past the coverings of life's circumstances and found that if I look hard enough, there is a divine gift, wrought by a loving Hand and over-shadowing Presence.

Just know that you are my friend—not as the world terms friendship—and my profound respect and love for you run deep. I believe that whatever time people share with one another, be it five minutes or a lifetime, we are a part of each other's lives. I am so blessed to be part of yours. Thank you for all your caring and for using your God-given gifts to help keep me alive. I thank God, too, for allowing me to continue doing the work He has given my hands and heart to do for His glory. I pray that God will continue to bless you and your family, keeping you safe in your spirit, soul, and bodies, and that He will nurture you and yours at the level of your deepest needs.

Love, in Christ Jesus,

Carole.

Are there any explanations or answers as to what happened? I don't know. When we spoke, the doctor was very touched by my letter, but he had no answers. God does, and although He hasn't divulged them to me, I am so thankful that He healed me one more time.

It Is Well with My Soul

I am the Vine and My Father is the Vinedresser. Any branch in Me that does not bear fruit [that stops bearing] He cuts away (trims off, takes away); and He cleanses and repeatedly prunes every branch that continues to bear fruit, to make it bear more and richer and more excellent fruit.

—John 15:1, 2 (AMP)

When peace like a river attendeth my way and sorrows like sea billows roll. Whatever my lot, Thou hast taught me to say, It is well, it is well with my soul. When Horatio Spafford penned the words to that beautiful song, it was after having suffered the loss of his entire family in a shipwreck. I cannot imagine the depths of his pain and yet, his focus was not on the external circumstances of his life, but rather on things eternal. He put the emphasis where it should be by adding, *Though Satan should buffet and trials should come, let this blest assurance control, that Christ has regarded my helpless estate and hath shed His own blood for my soul.*

Though the song, *It Is Well With My Soul,* has for many years been one of my favorites, when I began working on this chapter, I realized those words have greater meaning for me than ever before. For many weeks I could not write anything, and it seemed as though I had come up against an invisible brick wall. It is not that the accumulated trials of life had caused me to lose faith, nor was my walk with God not right, but it seemed the closer I got to Him, the more I was aware of my "helpless estate," as Spafford put it.

Although I loved God more than ever before and no longer had the need to question Him as to why things are the way they are, in recent months I had become increasingly aware that something was wrong with my heart attitude. I realized it was much easier to teach godly principles than to put them into practice in my daily life. Despite all the outside work I was doing in His name, on the inside I knew it was *not* well with my soul.

I began to examine my motives in everything I did—even to the writing of this book. Was it to have you, dear reader, get to know and love me more? God forbid! If that were the case, I have entirely missed the mark. Instead, I pray with all my heart that it has provided you with faith-building encouragement and the realization that God is meant to be, and *can be* glorified through every one of our life experiences.

Every day I felt the Holy Spirit tugging at my heart, making me intensely aware of my thought life. When I listened to what was going on inside, I didn't always like what I heard. What was even worse, I had the distinct feeling God didn't like it either. I became acutely conscious of my need to love God more and to truly begin loving other people the way He loves me. It was as though He was saying to me, "Clean up your act, Carole. It's time to grow up."

I'm sure many of you can relate to what I am saying. Everyone with whom I have shared these thoughts has felt the same way. There is no doubt God is doing a work in His Church. There is an inner cleansing going on such as never before. Most of the brethren have the feeling that we are very near the end of this period of grace and are on the thresh-hold of great changes in the world and in our comfort zone. I believe these changes will usher in a mighty move of God.

It is true that no one knows exactly when Jesus is coming back for His Bride, the Church. However, the way things are shaping up would lead us to think it is not too far off. In the meantime, the Holy Spirit is doing a fine-tuning within the body of Christ. He is preparing us for things to come, not only making it possible for us to withstand the onslaughts of the enemy in the last days, but He is also enabling us to do greater things for the Kingdom now. I'm excited! I feel as though I'm living out the above verses in John 15. Dead branches are being cut off, and we are being continually pruned so we will bear more abundant and excellent fruit. Although I'm excited about it, I don't like being pruned. It hurts.

In the Introduction to this book I wrote it was important for me to remember that the most significant things in my life were not those which happened or what I learned through my intelligence, but what God has written on my heart. During this time of spiritual cleansing, I had to look deep into the very core of my heart to see what else was written there. Once more, I found myself asking many questions.

"What is going on inside of me, Lord?" I asked. "What tenants, what old pains, disappointments, and unforgivenesses are still lodging in the small, dark regions of my soul because I have given them the legal right to stay? Why is it that small sparks still have the power to ignite great blasts of fury from within? What fires are still smoldering deep inside? What living contracts are still in force there? Whom have I not forgiven? What have I not released to You?" As David did in the Psalms, I asked Him to search my heart and expose the hidden sin.

Strangely enough, each time I attempted to dig deep within, I felt something I was unable or unwilling to identify. I wanted to run, but in spite of the terror, I plunged forward. Finally, I came to the realization that lurking somewhere in the intimate recesses of my soul was a mountain of pain sitting there, high and untouched. Not only was there pain, but a lingering issue of disappointment with God. "Oh Lord," I moaned, "don't tell me I'm back there again. Don't tell me I still have unforgiveness." Eventually, the time came when I admitted to Him, "I can't even go there, God. I can't deal with it, whatever it is. Not now, anyway. I'm not ready. I really need Your help."

Every time I felt myself getting close to making contact with that inner mountain, I felt like the Israelites in the book of Exodus must have felt when they approached Mount Sinai. I was afraid that if I came too close and even touched it, I would die. Dying is not an easy thing. Whether it is physical death or dying to self, it is still difficult. In one way, what I was feeling was a healthy fear warning me of danger. However, the enemy was also using it as a hindrance to my being set free and going forward with the Lord. Being both afraid and not knowing how to go forward, I had to leave it in God's hands and wait on Him.

Several days later I happened to go out into my garden to drink in the beautiful changes taking place and to bask in the warmth of the lovely Indian summer afternoon. I gazed at the leaves, whose beauty and colors were being brought out in such magnificent splendor. "It's not so different from what You do with us," I said to God. "Just as the leaves turn more beautiful as they die, as we die to self, You allow our inner beauty to come forth as well." I listened to the birds singing and laughed as I watched a squirrel stuff his fat little cheeks full of acorns as he tried to carry an armful of them to his nest. Then, completely out of season, I saw a butterfly. I love them—not only for their beauty, but because for me they are symbolic.

My mind wandered off as I thought about the many ways our lives parallel the butterfly's life cycle. When it is born, it is nothing more than a helpless little caterpillar, totally dependent and totally engrossed in fulfilling its needs. It crawls around on a leaf and begins eating and consuming everything in its immediate surroundings in order to grow. Then, as its life progresses, it wraps itself in silk as it builds a cocoon and withdraws from the world. There it is kept until, in the fullness of time, it finally emerges, revealing incredible changes that have taken place. It is no longer a caterpillar, but a butterfly—the same entity, but a different expression of its nature.

So it is with man. When we are born we are totally dependent on others, constantly needing to be fed and nurtured in order to grow, solely engrossed in our self-will and self-interest. To prove this point, observe any two-year-old, and you will hear them repeatedly say the word *Mine!* Children truly believe everything in the world revolves around them. This is why they are so profoundly affected when their surrounding circumstances go awry. They believe they are the cause of the problem because they see themselves as the center of all things and therefore assume the blame.

However, hopefully this changes as man grows and begins to mature. Eventually we come to know that there is Something or Someone greater than ourselves out there Who is drawing us. We hear the call of God and it is as though He plucks our spiritual heartstrings and something deep within us resonates. He whispers to us, "Seek My face," and our heart says, "Thy face will I seek, oh Lord." In time we, too, begin to close ourselves off from the things of the world. As we read the Bible, we become enfolded in the silk of God's Word as it becomes our cocoon to keep us until that day when He calls us forth to fulfill that purpose for which we were created.

Just as the butterfly struggles in order to emerge from its cocoon and needs the struggle to strengthen its wings for flight, so must we endure the hardships and trials of life in order to strengthen our spiritual wings. When we emerge we are the same entity, but a new creation in Christ. Behold! All things are made new!

Once the butterfly takes wing, its sole purpose is to mate and reproduce and then it dies. So it is with us. We "take flight" by bearing spiritual fruit for God and seeing Him reproduced in our lives and in the lives of those who come after us. We, too, must accept His invitation to become One with Him. Then He brings forth new life in and through us, as we are willing to die to self.

This last thought brought me back to the reality of where I was and of the task before me. I was still frightened. I told God, "All I can do is trust You, Lord. Apart from You I can do nothing, so please, get to the core of what is still inside of me. You do the pruning. Whenever You think I'm ready, Lord, please do it." I suspended all my usual activities and spent several days quietly waiting on Him and seeking His face.

When the pruning did come, and He opened that reservoir of pain, I felt as though I would die. At first I thought I would never be able to stop crying, but after I released the pain and unforgiveness in my heart, I was able to go forward and walk with a lighter step in the newness of life in Christ Jesus. However, I know this pruning is probably just one of many yet to come. Although I shudder at the thought, I can still smile and say, "It's okay, Lord. Bring it on. You've brought me this far, You're not going to forsake me now."

The last verse of Spafford's song says *And Lord haste the day when the faith shall be sight. The clouds be rolled back as a scroll. The trump shall resound and the Lord shall descend, even so, it is well with my soul.* Despite the fact that God has added years to my life and life to my years, how I look forward to that great and wonderful day.

Meanwhile, what is the Holy Spirit saying to us? He is telling us the fields are white to harvest. That means there are billions of people ripe and ready to hear the message of salvation. In Romans, Chapter 10, we are asked, "How will they hear unless somebody tells them?" The time is short, and the Lord has allowed us to be here at this specific time in history to be a part of His plan and purpose for this generation. We have to do it and, with His help, we can. He is calling us to be bold, strong, and courageous. He is calling those whom He chose and set apart to be holy before the foundation of the world, before time itself. That's you and me.

I believe there is a call to holiness such as never before. God not only wants us to grow in our love for Him, but He also wants us to reach out to others who desperately need to hear the message of His love. I thank God I heard it. He graced a moment of my life with His presence and it has never been the same. That was not the end, however. It was the beginning of a life-long process called "sanctification."

Now we are being pruned because there is a dying world out there, hungering for the spiritual food, the more excellent fruit, we have to give them. They are thirsting for a sip of the Living Water from the Well of Salvation. God intended for us to be the ones to bring it to them. Jesus told Peter, "Feed My sheep." (John 21:16). He is saying the same thing to us today, and I don't think He is interested so much in what we have done for Him in the past as much as what we are going to do. Whenever I ponder why God has kept me here, I know it is not only to fulfill His plan for my life, but also for the lives of those whom He has touched and will continue to touch through me.

My life has certainly been an interesting one and, although there is still room for improvement, I have learned much. Namely, that I cannot do anything without God's help, and each day I need to keep asking for more grace. I've learned that He never leaves us nor forsakes us, and He can change our setbacks into comebacks. When there seems to be no way out of a problem, God always makes a way— not just so we can *go* through them, but that we can *grow* through them. I found He doesn't call the qualified, but He qualifies the called, and what He calls us for, He equips us for.

Every day I pray to grow in wisdom, in years, and in favor with God and man, and He has faithfully answered that prayer. My faith in Christ has not been a one-time choice, but a lifetime challenge. I learned that contentment is not having everything I want, but being satisfied with what I have. I have stopped looking at what I've lost and have looked at, and been thankful for, what I have left. I have been able to not dwell on the pain, but to look at what blessing of eternal value was being worked out through it. I have learned to not let my disappointment turn into bitterness, and then I've learned to thank God, whether I understand what is going on or not. This attitude of gratitude is what has enabled me to praise God continually and give Him the glory through every circumstance of my life. There is no other way.

I have learned the value of being a cheerful giver and found that the more I give away, the more He gives me to give away; the more I give of my time, the more time I have to give; the more I love, the more He blesses me with love.

When I look around me at the beauty of this world, I know it but masks a little bit of heaven. Although I deeply love my family and friends, I have learned to hold them loosely as one would hold a bird. I have stopped saving things for a special occasion, because every day I'm alive *is* a special occasion. I try to keep a healthy balance in my life. I allow myself to cry when I feel the need, yet I love to have a good belly laugh and do that a lot. I still plan for the future, but I do not worry about what tomorrow might bring. Although I rigorously pursue God with all my heart, I know there is nothing wrong with just plain having fun.

There is never a time I am not aware of being in God's presence, not only when I am in good fellowship with Him, but even when I mess up or lose my patience. Then I know I can always turn to Jesus and ask for, and receive, forgiveness and mercy. I have also learned the incomparable value of those quiet moments I spend with Him. They are times of refreshing and like sips of Living Water to my parched soul. With the Holy Spirit strengthening and nurturing me at the level of my deepest needs, I have learned to trust, persevere, and rejoice in God. Most of all, I have learned to look beneath the seemingly hard and ugly coverings of life to find the divine gift wrought by loving hands, enabling me to say, "It is well with my soul."

If I were to sum up my life in one sentence I would say, "By the grace of God, I am an overcomer." What He has done for me He can, and will, do for you. Scripture tells us that God is able to do exceedingly abundantly above anything that we could ever ask or think. If you stay in His Word, He will continue to lead and guide you from victory to victory. Believe that God loves you and learn to have godly fear. Be quick to forgive and be open to receive forgiveness. Pray for wisdom, discernment, holy boldness, and a closer, obedient love-relationship with Him.

He doesn't care where you've been, He will meet you right where you are. He sent his Son to pay for our failures, so when the day comes that we face the Righteous Judge, He will look over the record of our sins and ask us, "Guilty or not guilty?" If we have accepted Jesus as our Savior, He will step forward on our behalf and say, "Father, this is one of Mine." Then the Father will say to us, "On the record of the sinless life of my Son, Jesus, and because of the blood that He shed for you, I not only forgive you, but I completely absolve you of all your sins. Welcome, My blessed child, into My everlasting kingdom which was prepared for you before the foundation of the world."

Are you there? Have you received Jesus and the gift that was purchased for you at the Cross? If not, I beg you to do it now. He is *longing* for you to do it. It's not too late—it's never too late with God.

Epilogue

𝒟ear Reader,

Throughout this book you have read the words *saved, salvation prayer, giving your heart to the Lord,* and other phrases relating to the same message. Some of you may not be totally sure of what is meant by those terms. This epilogue is to bring you to a complete understanding of what is being referred to, and to give you the opportunity to enter into that same relationship with the Lord Jesus Christ as those who have already done this.

It is the desire of God the Father that no man should perish. He wants all men to come into the knowledge of the truth that there is but one Mediator between God and man, and that is His Son, Jesus Christ. The message of the Bible is very clear. In Romans 3:23 we read that *all have sinned and come short of the glory of God*, and Romans 6:23 says, *the wages of sin is death.* This does not refer to physical death, but spiritual death, which is eternal separation from God. The good news is, that verse goes on to say, *but the gift of God is eternal life in Christ Jesus our Lord.* John 3:16 tells us, *God so loved the world that He gave His only begotten Son, that whosoever believes in Him shall not perish but shall have eternal life.* In other words, because of His love for us God gave His Son, Jesus, as a sacrificial substitute. He took the punishment we deserve.

We live in something called a time continuum, because time continues. However, before the foundation of the world and before time itself, it is as though the Father Almighty took countless millions of parts of Himself and set them aside to be holy. Then, in the fullness of time we were born. When He called to us by His grace, His unmerited favor, we responded.

In our limited capacity, we view our lives as one would watch a parade passing by—one segment at a time. However, from His perspective, God sees the entire parade from beginning to end. He looked over the whole of eternity and saw all the sins of man, beginning with Adam and ending with the last person on earth. He saw your sins and mine. The Father then pointed to a place in time and said, "This is where I will send My Son to dwell among them. He will clothe Himself in humanity so that some day they may clothe themselves with Deity. On Calvary's hill, My Son will take on all the sins of mankind and suffer their punishment. If they believe on Him, and on His work of mercy, they will be 'saved' from eternal death."

There are several places in the Bible which tell us that those who accept Jesus as Savior and Lord have their names written in a book referred to as either the Book of Life, or the Lamb's Book of Life (Phil. 4:3; Rev. 13:8; 20:12; 20:15). Revelation 21:27 informs us that only those whose names are written in that Book shall enter into the heavenly Kingdom.

The Bible tells us in Romans 10:9-10, *if we confess with our mouth the Lord Jesus Christ and believe in our hearts that God raised Him up from the dead, we will be saved; for it is with the heart man believes unto righteousness and with the mouth confession is made unto salvation.* The key is believing in our hearts, and confessing, which means to "say again." It is also important to believe Jesus rose from the dead, because His resurrection validates everything Jesus said about Himself. In other words, if you believe in Jesus and His resurrection, you will *tell* someone. It is not a matter of simply knowing *about* Jesus. Many people know about Him. In fact, even the devil knows about Him, and he's still a devil. Neither are we talking about having a form of *religion*, but what is being spoken of here is believing and trusting in, leaning and relying on, loving, and having a *relationship* with Jesus.

How do we do that? There is a simple way. The first step is to acknowledge our own sinfulness before God. I have heard many people say, "I'm a good person. I've never killed anybody. I don't hurt anyone. I've never stolen anything," or similar statements. This kind of prideful attitude blocks the grace of God. The truth is, we have all hurt someone, and whatever we have done to someone else that we would not have wanted them to do to us, is sin. Not giving God the glory He deserves is also sin. Therefore, if we are honest with God and with ourselves, we will admit our sinfulness and recognize our need for forgiveness.

Put as simply as possible, accepting Jesus as our Lord and Savior means that *in our heart* we acknowledge that He is truly God and that by His death on the Cross He paid the penalty for all our sins. Then, we have to come humbly before Him and receive the gift of salvation that was purchased for us at the Cross. If you have never done that, once more, I beg you to do it now, and offer the following prayer:

"Father God, in the name of Jesus, I come before You. Jesus, I believe You died and paid the price so that I might have eternal life. I repent of all my sins and ask You for forgiveness. Please come into my heart and send Your Holy Spirit to lead and guide me into all truth. Teach me to love You more each day. I receive You now as my Lord and Savior. Thank You, Lord Jesus. Amen"

With all my heart I pray you were able to say that prayer with me. Perhaps it was not the first time. Perhaps you needed to rededicate your life to the Lord. What is important is that you *said* it, and you *meant* it. Tell somebody, and then rest in the knowledge that someday you will see Him face to face as He welcomes you into that eternal life of peace, love and joy prepared for you before the foundation of the world.

Be blessed and, in turn, be a blessing to someone else.

Carole Rucci

Mail Order Form

If you would like to order additional copies of *It's Never Too Late with God* or would like to be on a mailing list to receive information regarding upcoming retreats, books, or tapes by Carole Rucci, please use this form or contact:

Fight The Good Fight Ministries, Inc.
P. O. Box 94
Rockville Centre, NY 11571-0094

❏ **Check here for information on upcoming retreats.**

Please send (_____) copies of *It's Never Too Late with God* @ $11.00 each. I have added $1.50 postage and handling for each book.

Total Enclosed $_____

Please send check or money order to:
Fight The Good Fight Ministries

_____
Name

_____
Address

_____
City   State   Zip

Considerable price reductions will be given when books are ordered in quantities. For more information, or to order *Fight the Good Fight*, please contact us at address above, or e-mail your request to: fgfwjc@aol.com